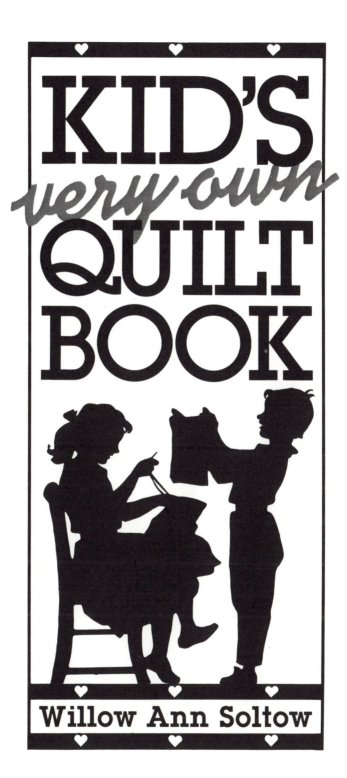

KID'S
very own
QUILT BOOK

Willow Ann Soltow

Front Cover and All Four-Color Photography:
    Perry L. Struse, Jr.

Cover and Interior Design:
    Geri Wolfe Boesen
Layout and Quilt Diagrams:
    Anthony Jacobson
Black-and-White Photography:
    Vicki Parker

Library of Congress Catalog
Card Number 85-051708

ISBN 0-87069-469-3

10   9   8   7   6   5   4   3   2

Copyright © 1986
Wallace-Homestead Book Company

Published by

Wallace-Homestead Book Company
580 Waters Edge
Lombard, Illinois 60148

One of the

Companies

For Bill and Shirley Soltow.

♥   ♥   ♥

Contents

Introduction

A quilt is a little like a diary. It tells whether its maker was careful or hurried. It tells if she liked the warm colors of yellow, red, and brown, or cool colors such as blue, gray, and green. A quilt's mistakes tell how adventurous the maker was willing to be as she combined different fabrics and colors.

Do you love bright colors? Does the sight of colorful calicoes make you smile? Do you like working with your hands and being able to say "Look what I did!" If your answer is yes, then quilting is for you!

The art of quilting is not difficult. If you can handle a needle and thread, you're already halfway there. In pioneer days, American girls learned to quilt at the age of five or six. Have you ever tried to imagine how people lived in those times when almost everything you needed grew in the woods and fields? Life was not easy. Even young children worked hard sewing quilts, shearing sheep, herding animals, and hoeing the garden. Pioneers used quilts for warmth in the wilderness, but today you can use the craft of quilting just to have fun.

I began quilting when I was fifteen and in my sophomore year of high school. My ancestors were pioneers in the backwoods of Pennsylvania. For years, I slept under layers of quilts made by distant relatives. I also was influenced by a few pages in a book called *Old Patchwork Quilts and the Women Who Made Them*, by Ruth Finley. It told a romantic tale of the days when people gathered to sew quilts all day, shared a delicious supper, and then danced together in the evening hours. Over and over I read the few pages about the old-time quilting bees. I daydreamed about who would share my quilts and my life one day.

Someday someone will share the quilts and quilted projects that you enjoy making from this book. That's the nice thing about quilts! First tries at other hobbies are often thrown away or hidden in the bottom of a closet. But a quilt—even a first quilt—is always special. It is always useful, and even its mistakes cannot make it seem less beautiful.

Quilts That Just Happen

Sometimes quilts are carefully planned. Sometimes they just happen. My first quilt seemed to happen all by itself. I began by embroidering a little square patch with a fish design. That led to a patch with an embroidered heart, which led to something else, and so on. It just fell into place on its own.

You won't have to rely on such luck as you follow the project plans in this book. There's room to experiment with shapes and colors, but you won't have to worry about whether this patch or that one is too big or too small. All of the measuring and figuring has been done for you. When your first quilt is done, perhaps it won't show quite as many mistakes as mine did. I expect you will be just as proud of yours as I was of mine.

The author's first quilt

The author's first quilt

The traditional Flying Geese pattern forms a fun border for this wall hanging, while the pillow is a variation of the Nine Patch.

Appliquéd schoolhouses and hearts are reminders of the days of one-room schools.

An appliquéd star and heart-stitched Nine Patch make pretty patchwork potholders.

Appliquéd hearts and lots of soft stuffing make a pretty, puffy case for eyeglasses.

A fabric checkerboard is made from the same stitching techniques as the traditional Nine Patch.

This quilt is a colorful test for all your patchwork know-how.

Detail of Autumn Leaves quilt.

Detail of Autumn Leaves quilt.

Detail of Autumn Leaves quilt.

In different areas of the country, the pattern for this single bed quilt has been called Bear's Paw, Duck's Foot in the Mud, and Hand of Friendship.

13

Decorate a design-your-own quilt with animals and mountains to create a favorite scene.

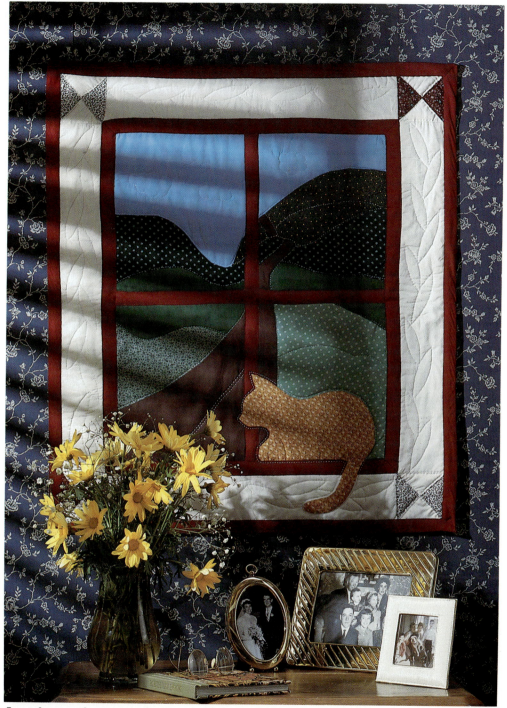

An advanced project, this cat in the window gives you a chance to perfect your appliqué skills.

Simple squares and rectangles are easy to stitch into this Amish mini quilt.

Quilts and Folk Art

Don't worry about being inexperienced when you start quilting. Our pioneering ancestors didn't! Many of their crafts, including their quilts, have a less-than-perfect look about them. This is what makes them interesting. It's what makes them folk art too. Willa Cather, a writer, called it "that irregular and intimate quality of things made entirely by the human hand." Today, we might call it "personalized."

Don't be afraid to let your hands guide you—even if they make a few mistakes. You can think of yourself as a kind of inventor as you go along. In the end, your quilt will be that much more beautiful—because you designed and sewed it yourself.

Decisions, Decisions . . .

As a quiltmaker, you will have many choices. You can make a quilt or a quilted wall hanging (a "mini quilt"). You might decide you don't want to do a quilt at all, but would rather make a quilted project—a game board, a quilted vest, or a pillow, for instance. Whichever you choose, you will be making something that is yours alone. Your quilt project will be something that tells a little about you—because you made all the decisions on how to create it.

What kinds of decisions are those going to be? You might choose to use a traditional pattern. Or, you might want to design your own pattern. Either way, this book will help you as you go along. You will also make decisions about what colors to use, which shapes to work with, and the size of your finished quilt or project. Don't feel you have to make an exact copy of the patterns in this or any other book. Feel free to bring your own ideas to the plans offered here. The more of yourself that you put into your project—even if it is only by using your favorite colors—the more rewarding it will be when it's finished.

Experiment all you like, but be sure to use good quality tools and materials as you go. The supplies suggested here are inexpensive and worth taking the trouble and money to buy. Always try to use the kind of needles called for. Use needles called *sharps* for sewing the cloth shapes. Use shorter *betweens* needles for actual quilting stitches. Work with good thread and new fabric so that, as your quilt wears with time, some parts of it will not wear out before others.

Using This Book

This book will give you everything you need to follow through on the creative quilting choices you make. If you enjoy thinking and wondering about what a quilter's life might have been like in pioneer days, take a look at chapters "1 What's In a Quilt?" and "2 Quilting Traditions." Together we'll explore the reasons why people have always made and loved quilts and why a fascination with quilts is part of our American heritage.

If you can't wait to begin making your own quilt or quilted item, turn right to the "Projects Section" of the book. You'll find plenty of ideas to help start you off on a project that's just right for you. Be sure to read chapter "5 About Doing Pieced Work" or chapter "13 About Doing Appliqué," depending on the project you choose. For best results, you should also read the chapter "Before You Begin." If this book helps you to discover the fun of sewing creatively, then it will have achieved its goal.

What's In a Quilt?

What's in a quilt? Color, texture, a promise of warmth—these are the things that have attracted people to quilts and quilting through the years. Americans have been making quilts for more than three centuries. But quilting is even older than that.

The word *quilt* comes from an Old French word, *cuilte*. This, in turn, came from the Latin word *culcitra*, meaning "stuffed mattress or cushion."

The principle of quilting is simple. You know from camping or hiking outdoors that wearing several thin layers of shirts and a light sweater is warmer than wearing one heavy sweater. Warm air is trapped close to your body, keeping you comfortable. The same is true for quilts! Who was the first person to discover that several quilted layers of thin cloth were warmer than one layer of thick cloth? We'll never know. But the discovery was made a long time ago.

The earliest known example of quilting is not in the form of a quilt at all. It is in the form of an ivory statue. Made around 3400 B.C., the statue is of an Egyptian pharaoh wearing a quilted robe. The oldest surviving quilt was made in Italy. It is almost five hundred years old. That's a long time for a fabric bed covering to last! In Mongolia, archeologists have found a quilted floor covering made nearly two thousand years ago.

Egyptian figure,
C.3400 B.C.,
with quilted robe

When European soldiers traveled to the Holy Land during the Crusades (A.D. 1000-1300), they found that the Arabs wore quilted clothing under their armor. The quilted shirts gave the Arabs added protection in battle and made them more comfortable. The craft of quilting was just one of the many new things that the Crusaders brought back with them when they returned to their homes in Europe.

European men and women were eager to learn about quilting. By the 1500s, quilted clothing had become fashionable in Europe. Men wore quilted vests and jackets. Women wore fancy quilted petticoats. Sometimes their dresses were cut away in front so that their colorful petticoats would show. Imagine living in a cold, damp, stone castle during the Renaissance. Warm, quilted clothes must have been very appealing!

Bed coverings were also quilted for warmth. Castles as well as cottages were drafty places to live. Quilts were used as blankets. In addition, beds were draped with quilted curtains to keep out the cold. Women made their own quilted clothes, wall hangings, and bed coverings. Common people and nobles alike made quilts. In time, they would bring the craft of quilting with them to the New World.

European women wore quilted clothing during the Renaissance

Quilts in America

Do you like the smoothness of a handmade clay pot or the nubby softness of a handwoven scarf? Today, people have a special feeling about things that are made by hand. But in the days when almost everything was handmade, items made by machines were special! Even in those early times, though, quilts were important.

When the Pilgrims boarded the *Mayflower* in 1620, they were careful to pack plenty of food and supplies. It is likely that they brought their quilts, too. They needed those quilts! The winter weather of New England would turn out to be very severe. Even with all their supplies,

the newcomers were poorly prepared for life in the New World. Remember, there were no guidebooks to tell them what they would find here. Only half of the Pilgrims survived their first winter.

Colonial American homes were unbelievably cold and drafty in winter. Even as late as 1717, one man wrote in his diary, "My ink freezes so that I can hardly write by a good fire. . . ." People slept under *layers* of quilts trying to stay warm. The women spent many hours sewing quilts. They knew each new quilt would help to protect their families from the chill air that blew through cabin cracks on frosty nights.

The Scrap Basket

Often, a woman kept a basket of cloth scraps near a chair by the fire. When evening came, she sat and cut the scraps into squares, triangles, and other shapes. Then she arranged the shapes into patterns to be sewn into quilts.

It took plenty of fabric scraps to make one cover. But each scrap had a history all its own. Cloth had to be made by hand in colonial days. Flax seed was sown in spring. In autumn, the flax was harvested. Over the following months, it was made into linen by the family. In warm weather, the family sheep were sheared. The wool from the sheep was dyed, using fruits, bark, or berries. Then it was spun into yarn, and the yarn was woven into cloth.

Each scrap of cloth told a story of long hours of work. It was a tale of the seasons, as well, from spring planting, through summer growing, to fall harvesting. It sometimes took sixteen months to make flax into cloth! Wool took a little less time, but each scrap in the quilting basket was precious.

Colonial Americans often wore an article of clothing for many years before it wore out. They patched holes in a jacket or dress until it would hold no more patches. Then it was ready to be recycled. It was cut up and placed in the scrap basket. The basket might hold triangles cut from a brother's coat, red squares from Mother's everyday apron, or diamonds cut from a sister's Sunday dress.

Quilting Comes of Age

The British wanted the American colonies to purchase cloth and other goods from England, so they restricted clothmaking in America. By law, textile machines and skilled laborers could not be sent to the Colonies from Great Britain.

The American Revolution brought an end to English rule and British trade restrictions. By the early 1800s, fabric had become more plentiful—and quiltmaking grew to be an even more popular American pastime. People could now afford to buy cloth just for quilts, instead of having to rely on whatever was in the scrap basket.

Country fairs gave women a chance to show off their quilting talents. In those days, fancy sewing was one of the few ways women were allowed to be artistic. This was important—especially in a world in which women could not vote, often could not own property, and in which they were expected always to obey their fathers and husbands.

Quiltmaking was important to many women for another reason. It gave them a chance to show how they felt about things that mattered to them. Through her quilts, a woman could make a statement. It could be a statement about her religion, her family—even about the life she had left behind to go pioneering in the wilderness.

Many quilt patterns were named for Bible stories. Bible sayings were sometimes written in ink on pieces of cloth and sewn into a quilt. A quilt made of cloth scraps from the clothes of beloved relatives told of a quilter's family. During the westward migration, many pioneer brides decorated their drab sod houses with brightly colored quilts. The quilt patterns they sewed often remind us not of the prairies where these women lived, but of the forests, green hills, and fancy flower gardens they left behind.

The Flowering of American Quiltmaking

The 1800s have been called the time of the "flowering of American quiltmaking." It's easy to understand why. Some of our most beautiful quilts were made during this period. Making quilts was popular with women from all walks of life. Piecing a quilt top gave them a chance to show off their needlework skills. The quilting bee offered people a chance to spend time with their neighbors. In areas where the nearest homestead or farm was miles away, this was important.

Some women made traditional quilts. Patterns for these quilts often were handed down from mother to daughter. The cloth and colors changed, but the pattern designs stayed the same. Other women used their own original designs. Often these quilts had special themes.

In many ways, Americans were beginning to enjoy more leisure time. This sometimes showed in their quilts. Some quilts made at this time were fancy. A fancy quilt could be a kind of status symbol. It showed that one had time to sew pretty designs instead of work.

New Styles

Near the end of the 1800s, quilt fashions (like clothing fashions) changed. People no longer wanted to make pieced or appliquéd quilts. They made a new style of quilt called the crazy quilt. Crazy quilts were sewn from bits of fancy cloth and were covered with decorative thread-work or embroidery. Soft velvet, shiny satin, and rich brocade were used instead of solid-colored cottons and calicoes.

Crazy Quilt patch

Drawing: Willow A. Soltow

In time, however, people lost interest in crazy quilts, and quiltmaking itself lost its popularity. However, during the Depression of the 1930s, people again became interested in making quilts. This is how it happened. The Depression put many people out of work. To help create jobs for these people, the government started a special program called the WPA, or Works Progress Administration.

Under the WPA, roads were built, forests were planted, and books and plays were written. The WPA also helped people who were good at crafts. People who did quilting, weaving, wood carving, and basketmaking were encouraged to make and sell their crafts. The art of quiltmaking came back to life. Just as in pioneer days, though, the choice of fabric often was limited, since no one had the money for new or fancy cloth. Old-time quilts made of plain cotton and calico became popular again.

Girl sewing in the 1930s

Not for Women Only

Throughout American history, quilts have meant something special to women because making them offered an opportunity to be artistic or to show their feelings. Not all quilting was done by women alone, though. When Calvin Coolidge—our thirtieth president—was a boy, he was ill for a long time. To take his mind off his illness, his mother taught him to cut and sew fabric squares. He chose a pattern called Baby Blocks. Later, the squares that he had pieced together were sewn into a quilt that now is displayed in the Coolidge home in Plymouth, Vermont.

The Shelburne Museum in Shelburne, Vermont, has a complicated and beautiful quilt made by a man who fought in the Civil War. Injured in the war, he made the quilt while confined to his bed. Part of this quilt is made of triangles sewn together. The rest is made up of cloth shapes of people, horses, birds, hearts, and stars. This old quilt has an unusual, original design, and it has held up well in the more than one hundred years since it was made.

Today, one of our finest quiltmakers is a man named Michael James. His abstract quilt designs are colorful and beautiful.

Adventures in Quilting

Modern quiltmaking and collecting have become a real adventure for some people. Quilt collectors enjoy hunting for antique quilts. Sometimes these quilts have been described in old letters or diaries.

The art of quiltmaking has become adventurous, too. Some quilt artists make three-dimensional quilt sculptures. Others make quilted wall hangings out of very untraditional fabrics. They may use cloth made from metal or plastic.

You can discover old quilts as well as make new ones. Many antique quilts have survived the years. There may be a faded old quilt in your grandmother's attic waiting to be rediscovered. Or, maybe there are some quilts kept by the historical society in the town where you live.

Each quilt tells something about the person who made it, just as your quilt will tell something about you—your likes and dislikes, your favorite colors, and stitched into one corner, your name and personal information. Can you imagine historians in the future looking at your quilt with a magnifying glass? Perhaps they will say, "Hmmm, let me see . . . I believe this dates from the late twentieth century, don't you agree?"

Quilting Traditions

American women had many quilting traditions. Most of them were fun. However, some of them, as we will see, were not.

How would you like to have to spend part of every day sewing? How would you feel about it if you were only five or six years old? In pioneer days, girls were taught to sew as soon as they could hold a needle. Each day they had to do a *stint* or amount of needlework. A stint was usually one or two hours' worth.

As a girl, Martha Washington enjoyed the sewing lessons her mother gave her. In fact, she liked her sewing lessons better than her spelling lessons. When she grew up, she could sew better than she could spell.

In those days, many people believed that sewing was more important for a young woman than studying. Fortunately, some young women rebelled against that idea even in those early days! For instance, one girl stitched into her needlework, "Patty Polk did this and she hated every stitch she did in it. She loves to read much more." Perhaps sewing was not nearly so much fun in those days because young girls *had* to do it.

Everything that needed sewing was sewn by hand. Young girls practiced sewing on pillowcases and handkerchiefs. Each stitch had to be tiny, straight, and perfect. Otherwise, it was ripped out and done over again. When a girl was a good enough seamstress, she was allowed to choose the fabric to begin a quilt of her own.

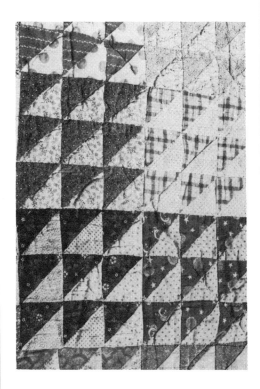

Nine Patch close-up

Her first quilt was often done in the Nine Patch design. This is one of the easiest patterns of all. (There are many variations on the Nine Patch pattern. Two are included in the projects of this book.) Some people believed that if a young woman slept under a new quilt or a bride's quilt, she would dream of the man she would one day marry.

By the time a young woman was seventeen or eighteen, she might well have finished twelve quilt tops for her hope chest. Often a girl married at this age. All her quilt tops were made into quilts at the same time. They were quilted with the help of her friends at a quilting bee. This was an exciting time for a woman. She would take the finished quilts with her to start her new life with her young husband.

A girl's thirteenth quilt often was called a "bride's quilt." It was always the fanciest, most beautiful one of all.

The Museum of American Folk Art in New York City is the home of a lovely, though mysterious bride's quilt. It is actually only a quilt top— since it was never quilted. Its maker worked long and hard sewing playful animals and curling vines. She made a block showing a young woman. She began a matching block picturing a young man—but never finished it. We know she began the block because her paper template (pattern) of the man's figure was found years later. The top was finished, not with the block that showed the man, but with another block that matched the rest of the design.

MAFA Bride Quilt detail

Drawing: Willow A. Soltow

What became of the quilter? No one knows. Perhaps her engagement was broken off. Perhaps she became ill and let someone else finish the quilt top. The figure of the man looks a little like a sailor. Maybe he was lost at sea. We can never know for sure.

Brides were not the only ones to need quilts. Freedom quilts often were made for a young man's twenty-first birthday. When he became twenty-one, a man could work for himself. Until then, his work and any money he made belonged to his father or family.

The Quilting Bee

Today many people make their quilts all by themselves. Years ago, though, having a quilt top to be quilted was just an excuse for a wonderful kind of party—a quilting bee.

Old-time quilts often were huge. They were designed to be warm, and they draped far over the edges of a bed. It took hours and hours to sew the pieces of one of these large quilts into a quilt top. It took even more hours to quilt it—that is, to sew the top, the batting, and the cloth backing together. Most women held a quilting bee to get the job done. They invited all of their friends to help.

Early Americans had many kinds of parties for the different chores that had to be done. They had candle-dipping bees, barn raisings, corn huskings, and wool shearings. Everybody pitched in and made the work go fast. For people who lived in the countryside, these gatherings were especially important. Sometimes, on a country farm, people did not see anyone except their own families for days at a time. Everyone looked forward to a barn-raising or a quilting bee.

What might it have been like to be snowbound for three weeks on end and not see anyone but your relatives? That is what happened to one pioneer woman. In the winter of 1841, she wrote a letter saying:

> We have had deep snow. No (wagon) teams passed for over three weeks, but as soon as the drifts could be broken through, Mary Scott sent her boy Frank around to say she was going to have a quilting. Everybody turned out. . . .

People wore their best clothes to a quilting bee. Women made special food. A quilting bee was an all-day event. Sometimes it even lasted several days. The women would arrive early in the day. From morning until late afternoon, they took turns working around a large quilting frame. The wooden frame held the quilt flat so it was easier to sew. As one or two quilters grew tired of sewing, others would arrive to take their places.

The women enjoyed talking while they stitched. Sometimes one would take time out from quilting to entertain the others. She might sing a song, tell a story, play an instrument, or recite a poem. With a little entertainment to keep it going, the quilting bee lasted all day. Sometimes more than one quilt could be finished.

When evening came, the last quilt was taken out of the frame. The frame itself was folded up or raised out of the way. The men began to arrive, and a feast was laid out on a long table.

When dinner was over and the dishes cleared, some people rolled up the rugs and moved the furniture to clear a space for dancing. Nearly always, there were one or two fiddlers or banjo players in the crowd. The musicians would tune their instruments and begin to play. In a room lighted by soft candlelight, the dancers faced one another in two long lines—men in one and women in the other. The two lines curved out the door of one room and into the next. People often danced far into the night.

Friendship Quilts

Years ago, making a friendship quilt was a popular way to tell good neighbors that you cared about them. To make a friendship quilt, a number of women each contributed a single block to a quilt. The blocks were sewn together. Then they were quilted by the entire group and presented to someone special.

A friendship quilt might be given to a town leader, a pioneer couple moving out West, a young man who had just come of age, or perhaps to a family that had lost their home and possessions in a fire or flood. The gift of a friendship quilt kept people warm in spirit as well as in body. It was a constant reminder to them of their good friends.

Friendship quilts are still a nice way to show you care about someone or something. Some group-made quilts are not done for people at all—but to celebrate an event. For instance, during the 1970s, a group of women from New York State made a Hudson Valley quilt to celebrate the clean-up of the polluted Hudson River. The finished quilt was hung in a public building for everyone to see. It helped to remind people of the importance of keeping this beautiful river clean. Other friendship quilts have been made by people to celebrate the history of a club, a town, or a state.

Many Hands Make Light Work

Perhaps you belong to a Scout troop or youth group that would like to make a quilt. Or, maybe your home economics or "survival skills" class at school is interested in making and presenting a friendship quilt to someone special. Where do you begin? As with any new project, start simple. If this is your first attempt at making a group quilt, you might want to make a small quilt to be hung on a wall, rather than a large full-size quilt for a bed. A smaller quilt is just as fine a gift as a large one, and it offers a good way to practice group sewing skills.

It may help to have your group elect a leader to assign different jobs to others. It is up to the leader to divide the work as evenly as possible. Each person will make a block. In addition, other jobs include buying supplies—batting and extra fabric for any borders and the backing of the quilt; sewing the blocks and borders together; basting the quilt "sandwich" of the quilt top, batting, and backing fabric together; and binding the rough edge of the quilt when it is finished.

It may help for the leader to have a special notebook in which all decisions and ideas about the quilt project are written. It helps to have everything in one place.

The leader will also have to set dates for blocks to be finished and for other jobs to be done. Every member should understand from the start that blocks and other tasks need to be finished on time.

Making a friendship quilt is a good way to learn about working with others. The group will have to make many decisions together. Some of these decisions are:

- Do you want to make a full-size quilt or a wall hanging?

- Is your quilt to be a gift for one person or is it to be given to some public institution?

- Do you want to make a traditional block-style friendship quilt—or some other kind of quilt or wall hanging?

- Will you have a special theme, such as scenes from your town, women in history, or your friend's favorite animals? Or, do you just want to let everyone make any kind of block they like? (Sometimes the best friendship quilts are the ones in which everyone just has fun making whatever kind of block they choose.)

- If you are making a block quilt, do you want the fabrics of the different blocks to match or will you let everyone choose their own fabrics for their blocks?

Friendship Quilt

- What color fabric will you use to *set* the quilt—that is, what fabric will be used for any borders that are needed?

- Who's going to take the photographs? (Everyone, including the person who finally receives the quilt, is going to want a photograph or two to remember all the fun that went into making it!)

One helpful resource for group quilting is the book *Many Hands: Making a Communal Quilt* by Elaine Miles (San Pedro, Calif.: R & E Miles, 1982). You may also want to see if you can find an experienced quilter to help guide your group project. In any case, you'll find that making a friendship quilt is a wonderful way to learn about quilting and cooperation.

Name That Pattern

What are some of the things we can tell about a quilter just from looking at her quilts? Some old quilts were made slowly by careful people. They were sewn with tiny stitches. The tinier the stitches, the finer the quilt. Perhaps some of the makers of these quilts lived in splendid houses in a nineteenth-century town, where day-to-day life was a little easier than in the countryside. There was time for careful, fancy needlework.

Some quilts were made quickly by people who had little time for sewing. They may have had a family to feed and care for, gardens to plant, and farm animals to tend. Their quilts may have had big running stitches. Their seams were not always straight and perfect. But, nevertheless, they too are beautiful in their own way.

Just like quilts, quilt *names* also tell a story. Some patterns were handed down from a mother to her daughter and even to her daughter's daughter. Other patterns were one-of-a-kind. Still others were widely shared and copied. Throughout the history of quilting, women have traded quilt patterns. This sharing has kept alive many patterns that are especially beautiful or that tell of experiences that were once common to many people—like living in a log cabin, for instance.

Traditional pattern names tell us about history as it was really lived—and about the men and women who lived it. LeMoyne Star, Burgoyne Surrounded, and Washington's Quilt were named for American patriots. Pioneers who moved West designed the patterns called Kansas Troubles, Rocky Road to Kansas, the Cactus Flower, Prairie Flower, and Missouri Star. They

Lemoyne Star block

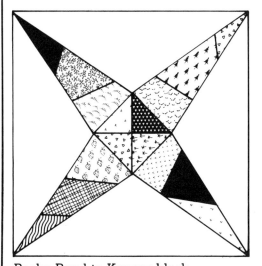

Rocky Road to Kansas block

Swing in the Middle block

Schoolhouse block

named quilt patterns after the houses they lived in, such as Log Cabin and Kansas Dugout. They even named patterns for the square dances they danced, such as Eight Hands Round and Swing in the Middle.

The Schoolhouse was a popular pattern. Teaching school was one of the few acceptable ways a single woman could earn a living. In addition, many pioneers took great pride in seeing that their children could read and write. A simple, one-room schoolhouse was found wherever there were enough families to pay for a teacher. The schoolhouse found its way into many quilts. (You'll find two among the projects in this book.)

The Bible was an important influence on pattern names. Biblical tales inspired The Palm Leaf, Crown of Thorns, Children of Israel, and Job's Troubles. The Delectable Mountains pattern was named for a famous religious book called *Pilgrim's Progress*. (Written by an Englishman in 1675, this book was still popular in America in the late 1800s!)

Pine Tree quilt

Rose of Sharon block

Early America was a farming society. Settlers cut down many forests. But they celebrated the beauty of trees, too, in quilt patterns like the Oak Leaf, the Maple Leaf, and the Pine Tree.

Can you picture a pioneer garden? There was so much work to do. The garden was mostly vegetables—the plants that people really *needed* for food. But in one small corner, a woman might raise a few flowers just to enjoy and help keep her spirits up. In the dark winter months, she'd remember those flowers by sewing a quilt like Rose of Sharon, Peony, Tulip, or Basket of Flowers.

Americans were surrounded by animals on farms and in forests. Some patterns were inspired by pets and farm animals like Cats and Mice, Goose Tracks, and Hen and Chickens. Other patterns told of wild animals. They included Bear's Paw, Flying Bats, Spider Web, and Snail's Trail. (To make your own Bear's Paw quilt, please see Project 6.)

Cats and Mice block

A Pattern of Your Own

How did our pioneer ancestors come up with so many different patterns? How did they think of the different names? They didn't do anything that you cannot do yourself. They looked around and created patterns from what they saw.

Old-time quiltmakers named their patterns for things they saw every day. They named patterns for plants, animals, stars, people, and buildings. Sometimes the names they chose for their patterns seem to fit those patterns very loosely. You have to use your imagination to see the animals in the Cats and Mice pattern. Other names, like Log Cabin, Windmill, and Palm Leaf fit their patterns almost too well. These pattern names sometimes call to mind the quilt pattern itself rather than the actual object. The Log Cabin pattern, for instance, is even sewn the way a real log cabin is made—with interlocking fabric "logs," one on top of the other.

The women who designed what we think of as traditional patterns began with simple shapes. They used triangles, squares, and diamonds. They arranged the same shapes over and over until they had a pattern they liked.

For instance, over the years, quiltmakers have come up with many variations on the Nine Patch. In addition, some patterns are easily changed into other patterns with entirely different names.

Try an experiment. Cut out a number of squares and triangles from heavy paper and arrange them—just to see what patterns you can make. If you like the pattern you come up with, try giving it a name. You may invent a quilt pattern that no one else has ever thought of before.

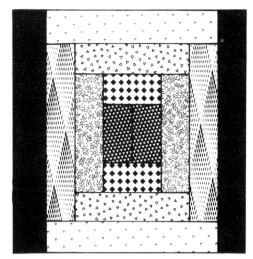

Log Cabin block

Real log cabin with interlocking corner logs

Quilts of Many Kinds

Patchwork was a familiar part of life for American pioneers. Each evening, while children slept in cold cabin lofts under layers of warm quilts, their mothers carefully mended the family clothing by candlelight. Nothing was wasted. Grown-ups wore their patched wardrobes for many years. Children often wore the patched hand-me-downs of older family members. Sometimes an article of clothing was completely taken apart and sewn back together into a "new" fashion.

Definitions

The term *patchwork* has been used by different people to mean different things. The dictionary tells us that patchwork is any needlework, such as a quilt, made from patches or bits of cloth. According to this definition, any quilt could be called patchwork.

Some quilters prefer to use the word patchwork to tell about a kind of quilting that combines the techniques of *piecing* and *appliqué*.

Piecing and appliqué are the two main methods of making American-style quilts. In pieced quilts, geometric shapes are sewn together edge to edge. In appliquéd quilts, cloth shapes are turned under. That is, the raw edge of the cloth is folded under about ¼" all the way around and sewn down. Then the cloth shape is pinned into place on a background fabric and appliquéd (or "applied") into place with hidden stitches.

Bear's Paw

Pieced Quilts

It is thought that when Europeans first came to this country, pieced quilts were more popular than appliquéd quilts. This may be true. Piecing let early quilters make use of many small scraps of fabric that might otherwise have been wasted. Not all early settlers used quilted bedding, however. Some probably used woven blankets or the skins and pelts of animals as bed coverings.

We can't know for sure just what kinds of quilts (if any) were used in colonial times. Few quilts from those days have survived. Household items were put to hard and constant use. This was true for quilts, too, and the earliest ones wore out long ago.

Bear's Paw pieced quilt. To make a quilt like this for your very own, see chapter 12.

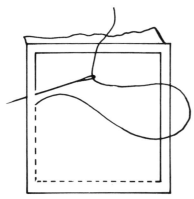

Running stitch

Pieced quilts are sewn with a stitch called the running stitch. A running stitch is just a basic up-and-down stitch that runs along close to the edges of two pieces of fabric, joining them together.

In piecing it is important to cut and sew pieces of cloth together accurately. If the cloth shapes are not exactly alike, it can ruin the whole quilt. That is why quilters cut their cloth shapes from templates before sewing them together.

A template is a shape made of cardboard or other stiff material, such as sandpaper or plastic. After you decide on the pattern you will use to make a quilt, trace and cut each of the pattern pieces from a piece of cardboard. If you need four triangles all the same size, make one cardboard template for all four triangles. Then place your template face down on the "wrong" side of the cloth—the side that will not show. Draw around the template edge to mark the shape on the cloth. (In this book, you will be using two templates for each shape. One is slightly smaller than the other. This allows you to mark a *cutting* line as well as a *sewing* line—but we'll get to that later.)

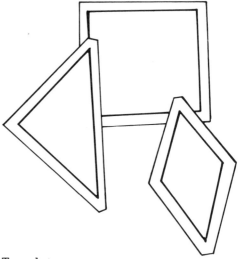

Templates

When all the triangles have been marked on the fabric, you are ready to cut the fabric. When each of the four triangles is cut out of the cloth, it should be exactly the same as the other triangles (if you've traced and cut carefully!). Next, the triangles (and/or other shapes) are ready to be sewn. Each is joined edge-to-edge to the next one. Before long, the whole pattern is completed.

Appliqué Quilts

More cloth is needed to make appliqué quilts than to make pieced quilts, because the cloth shapes are sewn onto a background fabric. Also, the shapes are usually fancier than simple squares, triangles, and diamonds. More fabric is wasted in cutting out fancy appliqué shapes, such as stars, hearts, flowers, and so on.

During the 1800s, appliqué quilts became popular. Families whose ancestors had come to this country a century earlier were now well established. They had enough money to buy cloth, and cloth itself was available and cheap. Many

Grapevine appliqué quilt block

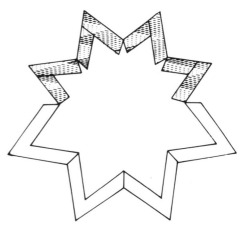
Turning under seam allowance

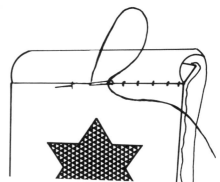
Blind stitch

quilters could afford to let their imaginations run wild in designing new quilt patterns. Although most still held a strong belief in "waste not, want not," they weren't as reluctant to use quilt designs that required wasting a little cloth.

Templates are used in making appliqué quilts just as they are in making pieced quilts. The template is cut from cardboard and placed on the wrong side of the cloth.

During cutting, a ¼" *seam allowance* is added all the way around the template. In *piecing,* this ¼" border is for sewing the shapes together. In *appliqué,* this *seam allowance* is turned under. The raw edges of each appliqué shape are folded under ¼" by hand. Some quilters even iron the folded-under part to make it stay that way as they sew. Either way, the appliqué is then sewn to the background material with matching thread and tiny stitches.

When all of the shapes for a single block or part of the quilt have been turned under and sewn, the shapes are ready to be appliquéd to a background fabric. They are pinned in place and sewn with a blind stitch—a stitch that comes up only in the crease of the turned-under edge of the shape. It is called a blind stitch because it is almost impossible to see.

What makes appliqué beautiful is also what makes it challenging—the hidden stitches that are almost invisible. Calico is a good cloth to use for appliqué shapes because the tiny print in the calico helps to hide any stitches that are too large.

You don't have to worry quite so much about your stitches showing in pieced work. Can you guess why? They are all made on the wrong side of the fabric—the side that does not show. The stitches in appliqué, however, show through on the right side of the fabric, so you have to be careful to make them as tiny as possible.

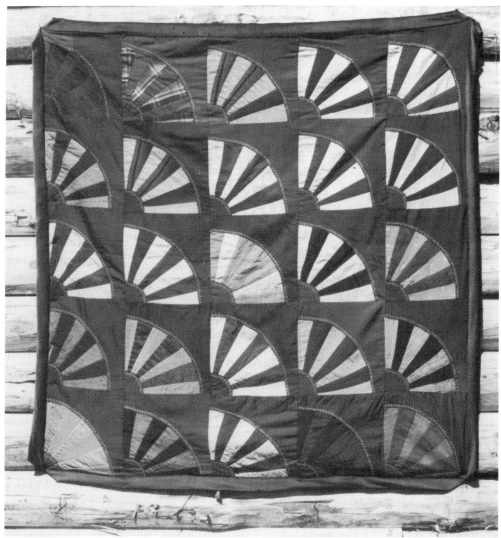

Grandmother's Fan patchwork quilt

Patchwork Quilts

When pieced work and appliqué join forces, the result is sometimes called *patchwork*. Earlier we learned that some people use the term patchwork to mean any kind of quilt. Others use it to mean a kind of quilt that is both pieced and appliquéd.

If you had a colorful pieced fan from the Grandmother's Fan pattern all pieced together—what would you do with it? You couldn't piece it to other shapes just like it. It isn't made for that. How would you solve the problem? You could turn under the outside edge of the fan all the way around. Then you could sew the turned edge as in appliqué. You could then pin the pieced, turned-under fan to a background fabric—a block, in this case—and sew it in place, using the applique or blind stitch. This would be an example of what some people call patchwork.

Special Names for Special Quilts

In America, quiltmaking truly became an art. Even a British writer said that "Americans set great store by their patchwork." She added that more importance was given to quilts in America "than in any other country. . . ."

With all of the attention on quilts in America, it is natural that Americans should have come up with some special kinds of quilts. Some of these styles of quilting began in America. Others began in other countries. They were brought here by immigrants—people from other countries who came to America to live. These people brought their own quilting customs from their homelands. Let's take a look at some of these special quilts and the techniques used to make them.

Crazy Quilts

Many people like quilts because of the soothing effect they have on the eye. In a busy, modern world, the sight of an old-fashioned quilt pleases people by reminding them of simpler days. One kind of quilt, however, is *not* soothing to look at. This is the crazy quilt. It can almost make you feel a little dizzy to look at one of these quilts.

Have you ever made a collage? A crazy quilt is a little like a collage made of material. It is made of pieces of cloth of different shapes, sizes, and colors. The pieces that make up a crazy quilt often are cut from fancy kinds of cloth, such as velvet, satin, or brocade. Usually, the cloth pieces are decorated with embroidery or fancy thread work. Sometimes ribbon, lace, or beads are also added.

Crazy Quilt block

The crazy quilt is thought to be the oldest type of American quilt. It was most popular during the last twenty-five years of the 1800s. This was during the Victorian era, when Queen Victoria ruled England.

A crazy quilt's different shapes of cloth may have been inspired by Japanese designs. Victorian Americans were fond of almost anything from Japan. The Japanese "cracked-ice" design may have given someone the idea for making the first crazy quilt, but no one knows for sure.

Most crazy quilts are made block by block. To begin a block, a piece of cloth is chosen as a foundation—something on which to build the rest of the design. This foundation fabric does not show. All the other pieces of fabric are sewn on top of it, covering it completely. The foundation fabric for each block is the same size as the finished block itself.

Once the foundation is chosen and cut to the correct size for a block, it is covered with bits of cloth. These cloth scraps are decorated with fancy stitching. There are lots of pretty embroidery stitches that can be used to decorate a crazy quilt. Some crazy quilts are even embroidered with little pictures of animals, birds, or flowers.

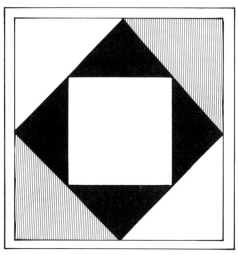

Amish quilt

Amish Quilts

Perhaps you've traveled through Amish country in Pennsylvania, Ohio, Iowa, or Indiana. Here you may have seen "the plain people," as they are called, riding in their horse-drawn buggies. They do not drive cars. Neither do they have telephones, electrical appliances, televisions, or radios. They do not go to the movies. Their entertainment comes from social/work gatherings, such as quilting bees and barn raisings. Their way of life is disciplined and simple.

Today, Amish women make quilts from all different kinds of patterns. But years ago, Amish quilts were very different from other quilts. For one thing, they were made only from the kind of fabric that the Amish used in making their clothing. This meant the quilts were mostly made of dark, solid colors, including blue, maroon, dark green, purple, dusty rose, and black.

Traditional Amish quilt patterns were strong and simple. Yet the quilting in them often was complicated. Usually Amish quilts were pieced rather than appliquéd. Amish quiltmakers considered appliqué, calico, and bright colors to be too fancy or "worldly" for the plain people. They made up for the simplicity of their designs with exquisite quilting stitches. Wide, solid-color bars, squares, and borders showed off the beautiful quilting that was done in black thread.

One of the most famous Amish quilt patterns is called Center Diamond. Large, bold pieces of cloth in only three or four dark colors are used. The large fabric pieces help to show off the careful quilting stitches.

Another pattern is called Sunshine and Shadows. Made up of many tiny squares, this pattern has rows of light squares followed by dark ones. It usually includes a wide border.

"Bars" is the name of a third quilt pattern. In this design, wide, up-and-down bars of solid-colored cloth form a large square. The square has a wide border.

Although these three patterns—Center Diamond, Sunshine and Shadows, and Bars—continue to be made by the plain people, today many Amish women make other kinds of patterns too. More and more, younger Amish women are turning to calicoes and tiny prints in making their quilts.

Arpillera

The Arpilleras of Chile

The name *arpillera* comes from the Spanish word for burlap. The backing fabric of an arpillera is a heavy, burlaplike cloth.

Arpilleras are made by women from South America—especially from the country of Chile. The arpilleras are made of small rectangles of appliquéd cloth, sewn together to form fabric pictures. Sometimes solid colors, sometimes calicoes and patterned cloth are used. The appliquéd pictures are nearly always decorated with brightly colored embroidery stitches.

Usually arpilleras show a scene of a town or the country. Sometimes they show a picture from the Bible. Small handmade dolls are sewn right onto the cloth picture.

The dolls in the arpilleras always look busy. Sometimes they are cooking in a large pot on a fire outside. Sometimes they are washing clothes and hanging them out to dry. Other times the dolls portray biblical scenes, such as the Nativity or Noah's Ark.

Today, the government in Chile is harsh. Some arpilleras are made to protest against the government. Others, though, are made simply to remind people of the goodness of everyday living.

Mola

The Molas of the Kuna Indians

The Kuna Indians live on the San Blas Islands off the coast of Panama in Central America. They are known for making colorful molas or fabric pictures. Molas are usually small squares, rather than large quilts. They are used to decorate clothing or as wall hangings.

The cloth used to make molas is always solid colored rather than patterned. Usually, the brighter the colors, the better. The patterns look like mazes of color. Often, the maze outlines a picture—a bird, an animal, or a star—for example.

The technique used to make a mola is like appliqué. In traditional American appliqué, you turn under the edges of a small piece of cloth and sew it onto a larger one.

A mola is made by doing "reverse" or cut-through appliqué. The first step in making a mola is to stack several layers of cloth. Each layer is a different solid color. Molas look as though they were made by stacking layers of cloth, then cutting through the top layers to expose the bottom ones. This may be how they look—but it is not really how they are done.

Actually, when making a mola, the design is drawn onto a layer of cloth. Then the design is cut and turned under. That layer is stitched to a solid background layer. Then one or more top layers are added afterward, each with the design cut a little larger to let the layers beneath show through. A mola may be made of many layers of cloth.

Pa ndau: The Needlework of the Hmong

Another kind of cut-through appliqué is made by refugees from Vietnam. These people escaped from their war-torn homes and came to this country for safety. They are known as the Hmong (pronounced "mung.") It is estimated that about 60,000 Hmong have settled in the United States over the past five years or so. The Hmong women brought with them their beautiful style of needlework. It is called Pa ndau (pronounced "pon-dow.")

Pa ndau is similar to quilting, but it does not have batting, nor is it quilted. It does use appliqué stitching techniques, and it looks like quilting from a distance.

The Hmong women, like the Kuna Indians, use cut-through appliqué to make their needle art. Unlike the patterns of the Kunas, however, Hmong needlework is usually made with well-balanced geometric designs—squares, triangles, and diamonds. (Molas, on the other hand, are not always symmetrical or perfectly balanced. In addition, molas often have picture shapes in them, while Pa ndau has geometric shapes.)

Hearts and Rings Pa nDau design from *Creating Pa nDau Appliqué*. Printed by permission of Carla J. Hassel.

Making Pa ndau is a little like cutting out a snowflake from folded paper. In Pa ndau, three layers of solid-colored cloth are used. The top layer is folded and cut like a paper snowflake. Then, the cut edges are carefully turned under and stitched to let a second fabric layer beneath show through. As in the crazy quilt, a foundation layer of fabric helps to hold the first two layers in place.

Sometimes embroidery around the geometric shapes is added.

Traditionally, the Hmong have used many different, bright colors to make their needlework. Since coming to the United States, many of them have begun using the colors of the American flag for their appliqué work. The colors red, white, and blue have special meaning to these refugees in their new homeland.

Before You Begin

Your first quilting project will be your introduction to a new art form. It will give you a brand new feeling of accomplishment. It will also give you a starting point from which to measure your progress as you become a better quilter. It is important to pick a first project that is right for you.

Nearly every quilter looks back happily on a first completed quilting project. Most of us end up being pleasantly surprised at how well our first project turned out. Quilting is one of the few crafts in which even a simple project can look terrific.

As you read through the steps for making quilt projects in this book, you will notice that the term *quilt* is used to mean many things. For our purposes, a quilt can be a full-size bed quilt or a quilted wall hanging.

Making the Most of Experience

This book is not meant to be a step-by-step course. Some people like to read carefully about a project before attempting it. Other people like to jump right in. This book is designed so you can read a lot or a little before beginning a project. Be sure, though, to read "5 About Doing Pieced Work" or "13 About Doing Appliqué," as well as "6 Quilting Makes the Quilt" before starting *any* project. For best results, you should also reread this chapter.

In quilting, as in many things, there is more than one "right" way to do the same thing. We will try to focus on the *easiest* "right" way to complete each project. The projects are labeled to help you choose what is best for you: "very easy," "easy," and "a little more challenging."

Start simple. If you have some sewing experience, but no quilting experience, begin with either of the two potholder projects—Project 1 or Project 7. Even if you've never sewn before, the pieced and appliquéd potholders will not be too difficult. Yet each contains all the elements of making a full-size quilt—except the size!

You may want to try a pieced or appliquéd pillow and, perhaps later, a wall hanging. (You'll just have to resist the urge to make a bed quilt as your first project.) Practice your quilting skills on simple projects first. It could make the difference between whether you enjoy your first try at quilting or whether you give up without giving the craft an honest chance.

If, on the other hand, you have some quilting experience, or if you have an experienced quilter to help guide you, you may want to begin with a more advanced project. If you are tempted to begin with a bed quilt, consider this: a smaller wall quilt will give quick, satisfying results. It will also give you a feel for the sewing skills used in quilt-making. Once you have made a wall quilt, you'll know if you have the time and patience needed to finish a larger project.

Planning for Time

The amount of time you have to sew is also important in choosing a project. Suit your project to the amount of time you have available. If you have some time to sew every day, you may want to try a larger project, such as a wall quilt. If not, maybe a smaller project is for you.

Choosing Colors

Once you have made your choice of a project, choosing colors is the next important (and most fun) step. Choose colors that you enjoy, since you will get to know them well as you sew. Think about these things as you choose your colors:

- If you want to use light colors, be sure the fabric is thick enough to hide folded under edges. Check by folding an edge over to make certain that the fabric underneath can't be seen from the front.

- Choose colors that have the same intensity. For instance, a bright red may look better when combined with a strong navy blue than with a washed-out light blue. Try holding different colors of fabrics together to get a feel for how they look together.

- If you do not feel confident about choosing colors that 'go well together, try one of two things: Use several shades of the same color—a pale pink, a deep rose, and a dark crimson, for example. Or, choose a two-color calico and use it with a solid color that matches the printed design. A green calico with tiny yellow flowers would work well with solid yellow cotton fabric.

- You might want to plan a wall quilt or a bed quilt with colors that go with the room in which the quilt is to be displayed.

- For pieced work, fabrics with small prints will look better than those with large prints—especially if the pattern pieces you use are small.

- For appliqué, be sure that your pattern pieces contrast or stand out well against the background fabric you have chosen for the quilt top. Contrast really means "to stand against." It is important that your fabric design stand out well in appliqué. It is for this reason that so many traditional appliquéd quilts were done in one or two colors on a white background.

- Most important of all, choose colors that you really enjoy. You don't want to grow tired of the colors in your project before you are done.

Materials

Good cooking and good quilting have something in common. It's best to get all your materials together before you do anything else. You wouldn't want to begin making a cake only to find that you had used up the last of the flour the other day. It's the same way with making a quilt. As you gather your materials together, keep these things in mind:

- Use good-quality fabrics and thread. Bargain brands sometimes are not a bargain. They can fade, run, or fall apart.

- When starting out, limit yourself to using colorfast, pre-shrunk cotton. Cotton-blend fabrics that have at least 50 percent cotton in them are also fine. If you don't know which fabrics these are, ask for help from the fabric store assistant. In addition, the label on the fabric *bolt* of new cloth will tell you if the fabric is pure cotton or a cotton blend (cotton and something else.) The label will also tell whether the fabric is colorfast and pre-shrunk. If it doesn't say these things on the label, don't buy the fabric!

Even though they choose colorfast, pre-shrunk fabric, many quilters wash their fabric before using it just to be sure it won't run or shrink if it gets wet. If you like, you can do this by washing your fabric in the washing machine or by hand until the rinse water is clear and shows no hint of color. If you are using fabric scraps and you don't know whether they are colorfast and pre-shrunk, you should wash them just to be safe.

- After you have tried one or two projects, you may want to experiment with fabric. Think about the following things: Choose fabric that has a firm weave rather than a loose weave. This is especially important in appliqué work. Cotton fabric with a firm weave is slightly stiff to the touch. Calico is

usually like this. Cotton knits, on the other hand, are an example of a loosely woven fabric. Try feeling the difference between the two the next time you visit a fabric store.

In general, stay away from heavy fabrics, such as corduroy, velvet, and canvas. These fabrics are made of cotton, but they are too hard to quilt. Always avoid thin fabrics. Fold over the piece of fabric you are considering and see if it shows through. With thin fabrics (as with very light-colored fabrics) the folded-over seam can show through on the front side and ruin the look of your quilt. Also, stay away from permanent press, knits, and fabrics that feel slippery to the touch.

- Use polyester or cotton batting for the middle layer of your quilt. It may be a little easier to quilt through polyester batting. In addition, polyester often looks better than cotton when it's washed. Unlike polyester, however, cotton has been used as a quilt batting for more than a century and a half. As some quilters point out—we don't know *what* polyester may do in the decades ahead!

- Choose a backing fabric just as you selected fabrics for the quilt or project top. Colorfast, pre-shrunk cotton is good. So are cotton-blend fabrics that have at least 50 percent cotton in them.

- Can you use a sewing machine? All of the projects in this book were designed to be sewn by hand. But if you want to join the pieces by machine in the pieced-work projects, go right ahead.

About Doing Pieced Work

P lease read this section before beginning any of the pieced projects (the first six in this book).

The Best Beginning

Before you do anything else, iron the fabric that you plan to use. If it is new fabric, iron out the fold that appears down the middle. If you are using scraps of fabric, iron them flat. This is not just to keep them looking nice. If your fabric is not ironed from the start, it will throw off the accuracy of your design as you mark and cut the fabric.

Cutting the Templates

To begin your quilt, you will need to cut out one or more templates. A template is a cutting or sewing guide. It is made of sandpaper, cardboard, or any other stiff, sturdy material. It is cut to the exact size and shape of the fabric pieces you will be working with. You will use it to trace onto the fabric. A template is made of something sturdy so that it will hold up while you use it to outline the fabric shapes you need. A template is needed to help you make all of the fabric pieces exactly the same size.

You will need a template for each different size and shape of fabric in the pattern you have chosen. For instance, in the Pinwheel block, there are two colors of fabric, but only one size triangle. To make this pattern, you will need only one template.

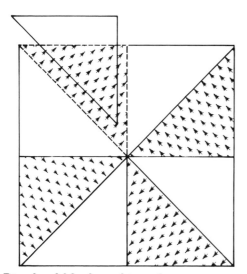

Pinwheel block and template

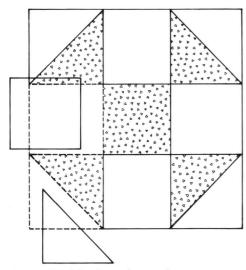

Shoo Fly block and templates

In the Shoo Fly pattern, there are two colors of fabric and two different shapes. To make this pattern, you will need two templates.

To cut out a template, follow the directions below. You will need tracing paper, pencil, and sandpaper or cardboard.

Step 1. If possible, use fine sandpaper instead of regular cardboard for your templates. The sandy side will cling to the fabric, and the template will not slip as you draw around it. Also, you will be less likely to mix up the right and wrong sides of your template. (The following directions are for making and using sandpaper templates. The back of some kinds of sandpaper is difficult to draw on with a pencil. You will not want to use this kind of sandpaper. If you cannot find the kind of sandpaper you need, make cardboard templates instead. Just be sure to mark the right side of your cardboard template so that you cannot get the right and wrong sides mixed up.)

Step 2. On each pattern piece in this book, there are two outlines. One is a thin outer line. The other is a thick inner line. For each pattern piece in your project, trace both outlines onto tracing paper.

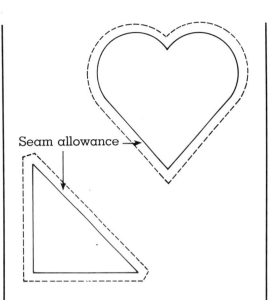

Seam allowance

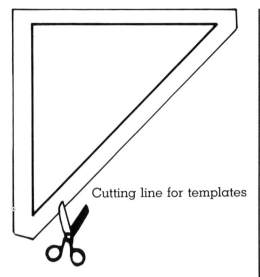

Cutting line for templates

The outer line that you trace for each template is a *cutting* line. The inner line is a *sewing* line. Most quilt pattern books give you a sewing line only. You are expected to guess at the cutting line and add it on your own. The templates in this book remove the guesswork. Cut on the thin line. Sew on the thick line of each pattern shape. The space between the two lines is called the seam allowance. This extra ¼" around the outside of the pattern pieces allows you to sew the pieces to one another. (Actually, adding your own seam allowance is not hard to do. You will find that using the special template drawings in *this* book is a good preparation for learning how to do this.)

Step 3. Turn your sandpaper sand-side down. (Or, your cardboard right-side down.) Turn the tracing paper over so the side on which you drew is facing down. Put the tracing paper on top of the sandpaper. Then retrace the lines you drew so that they transfer to the paper side of the sandpaper. Take away the tracing paper and darken the lines so they are easy to see. Do this for each different shape you need.

Step 4. Cut out the sandpaper templates carefully along the outer line that you have traced.

Step 5. Label each template with the name of your pattern and the number of that shape needed to make your pattern. If you need two different colors of the same shape, label the number of shapes needed for each color. For instance, you might label a triangle used to make the Pinwheel pattern this way:

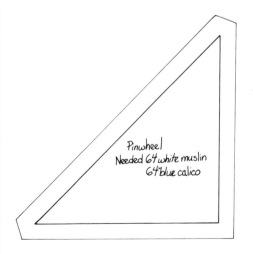

Pinwheel
Needed 64 white muslin
64 blue calico

Marking the Fabric

Now you are ready to mark or draw the lines on your fabric for cutting.

Step 1. Place your fabric right side down on a smooth surface. A table or clean floor is fine.

Step 2. Place the template sandpaper side (or right side) down on the fabric. Place it so that the template is laying with the grain of the fabric. If you are not sure what this means, look closely at your fabric. You will see that it is made up of many tiny threads going lengthwise and crosswise. "With the grain" means that the edge of the template is parallel to the selvage (finished) edge of the fabric. "Against the grain" means that the template is at a right angle to the selvage.

Saving fabric

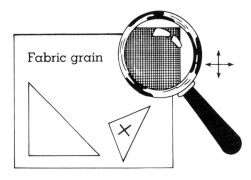

Step 3. Draw around the outside of the template with a pencil. Draw as many pieces as you need, keeping them as close together as possible to save fabric.

Step 4. Recut your template, cutting on the inner line. Discard the extra ¼" all around your template. Your new, recut template will now be exactly ¼" smaller all the way around than it was.

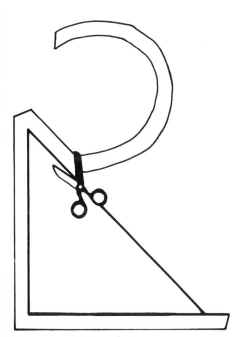

New, re-cut template

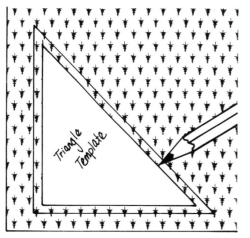

Tracing fold or sewing line

Step 5. For each fabric piece, place the new, recut template right in the center of the piece as you have drawn it. The template should be centered carefully. Now draw a line around the outside of the new, recut template. This will be your *sewing* line. The outer line, which you already drew, will be your *cutting* line. Just like the template drawings in the book, each of your fabric pieces will have two outlines when you have finished marking the fabric.

Cutting the Fabric

Step 1. Cut out each fabric piece, cutting carefully on the outer line you have drawn.

Step 2. As each piece is cut out, you may want to stack it with the rest of the pieces that are just like it. If a fabric piece has become rumpled, iron it gently once again. (Don't hesitate to use your iron often, but don't stretch your piece out of shape. Ironing is one of the great secrets of good quiltmaking.)

Sewing the Pieces

Step 1. As you sew your pieced blocks, you will work one block at a time. Begin by setting aside enough fabric pieces for a single block. Lay the pieces out to form the first block. You will want to sew the pieces together in the order given in the project instructions.

Step 2. To sew the first two fabric pieces together, line up the two pencil lines on either side of the two pieces. To do this, hold the two pieces with *right sides together*. Put a pin through the pencil line on the fabric piece facing you. Shift the second fabric piece until the pin comes out through *its* pencil line (on the side facing away from you.) Pin the two fabric pieces together with the pencil lines lined up as perfectly as possible. This means you will have to use the above method of putting the pin through the pencil lines in two or three places for each pair of fabric pieces. You will then use the pencil line as a sewing guideline.

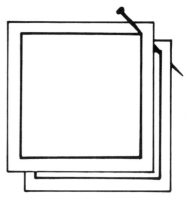

Pin-through method

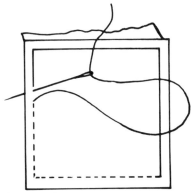

Running stitch

Step 3. Sew along the pencil line with a knotted, single strand of thread. Use a running stitch (a basic up-and-down stitch) to join the first two fabric pieces, right sides together. You do not need to match your thread to the fabric exactly. If you are using dark fabric, use dark thread. If you are using light-colored fabric, use light thread.

Step 4. Using the same method, sew together all of the pieces for your first block in the order directed in the project instructions. As you join the rows or groups of fabric pieces to others, be sure to line up the seams on the right sides of the fabric before pinning the right sides together. This is called "matching" the seams. This will help you to be sure the seams fall exactly where they belong when the block is finished.

Step 5. When your pieced block is sewn, iron it on the wrong side of the fabric. Do not iron the seams open as you would do if you were making clothing. Press the seams of light-colored fabric toward the dark pieces of fabric next to them, if possible.

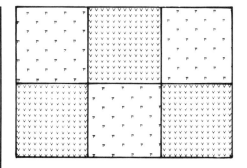

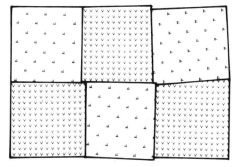

Matched and unmatched seams

Setting Your Quilt

Step 1. Depending on the project you are making, you may be working with more than one finished block. *Setting* means to sew all of the blocks together. To set the blocks, begin by laying them out just as they will appear in the finished quilt or project.

Step 2. Join the blocks in the order given in your project directions. When all of the blocks have been joined together, iron the finished piece, and you will be ready to begin quilting your quilt or project.

Quilting Makes the Quilt

Please read this section before beginning to quilt any of the projects. These instructions and quilting tips will help you do nice looking projects with the least amount of trouble.

Depending on the project you are doing, you will use one of two methods for guiding you in sewing the quilting stitches. Your project may call for sticking strips of masking tape on the quilt top to follow as quilting guidelines. The masking tape will not stick permanently to your quilt top. And it eliminates the need to draw straight lines on the quilt top with pencil.

On the other hand, your project may call for the use of quilting templates. These should be cut from regular paper (NOT from cardboard or sandpaper). They will be pinned in place and quilted around to form a design.

How To Quilt the Projects

Step 1. To prepare your quilt for the quilting hoop, measure the quilt top. Measure and cut the polyester batting or filling. It should be 2″ or 3″ bigger than the top on all sides. Measure and cut the backing fabric so that it is the same size as the batting.

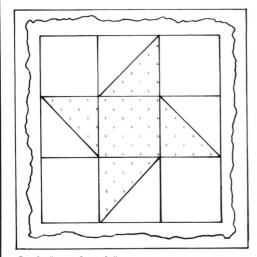

Quilt "sandwich"

Step 2. Now you are going to make a "quilt sandwich." Lay out the backing fabric (or lining) on a work surface (a table or clean floor). Place it on the work surface so that it is *right side down* and the wrong side is facing you. Next, lay the batting evenly on top of the backing. Place your quilt top *right side up* on the batting to complete the "sandwich." Be sure the top is evenly centered all around. The batting and backing should extend about 2" or 3" beyond the top on all sides.

Step 3. Use straight pins to pin the sandwich layers together about every 6" or so.

Step 4. You are now ready to fasten your quilt "sandwich" with basting stitches. A basting stitch is a long stitch about 1" or 2" in length. Basting stitches are removed before the project is finished. Their only job is to hold the "sandwich" together while you are quilting it. You might think the pins would be enough to hold the "sandwich" layers together, but they are not strong enough. In addition, it is too easy to stick yourself with a pin while you are quilting.

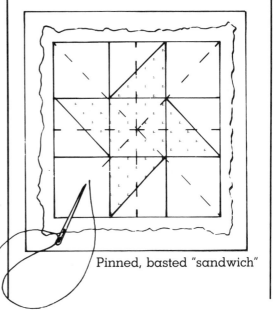

Pinned, basted "sandwich"

For these reasons it is best to *baste* the "sandwich" layers together as your project instructions tell you to do. Generally, a project is basted with four or more lines of basting stitches: one through the center from top to bottom, one through the center from left to right, one from the upper right corner to the lower left corner, and the last from the upper left corner to the lower right corner. Additional lines may be needed for larger projects. When the basting is done, remove the straight pins.

Step 5. The projects in this book are designed to be quilted on an embroidery hoop or a quilting hoop, depending on their size. Separate the two rings of your hoop. Place the quilt sandwich over the inner ring. Place the outer ring down over the inner ring. Tighten the outer ring so that the "sandwich" is taut or flat and does not sag.

Step 6. Tape the masking tape so that the edge falls where you want your stitches to show. Or, pin your templates in place with a straight pin.

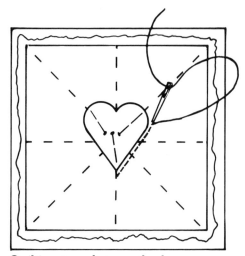

Quilting template method

Step 7. To do the actual quilting, you will be using a basic up-and-down stitch. Use quilting thread and a betweens needle. (Many quilters feel that the smaller the needle, the better.) Thread your needle but do not double the thread. Sew with a single strand. Make a knot in the end of one strand of the thread before you begin.

Bring the needle up from the underside to the top of the quilt. Pop the knot through the backing into the batting. Try to keep one hand on top and the other hand underneath the quilt.

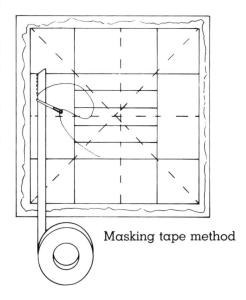

Masking tape method

Needle quilting

Many quilters pull the knot through the backing fabric and let it lose itself in the batting. But this is not absolutely necessary, if you find it difficult to do. The knot will not show if excess thread is trimmed and the knot itself is pulled firmly into the backing fabric.

As a rule, quilt ¼" *inside* pieced designs. Quilt ¼" around the *outside* of appliqué designs. Quilt directly around templates and beside strips of masking tape. Be sure that you do not quilt right to the edges of a project. On many projects, you will need about 1" of unquilted space all around the outside edge.

Right-handed quilters generally let their left hand do the work on the underside of the quilt and their right hand do the work on the quilt top. Lefties do the opposite. Try to take two or three stitches on your needle at a time—especially on straight lines of quilting—by holding your needle at a sharp angle. Still other quilters prefer to sew with just one hand, allowing it to move from underside to top and back again.

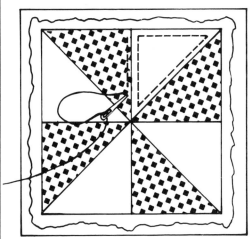

Pieced quilting

Appliqué quilting

This last method takes more time, but you may find it easier to use when you are just starting out.

How long should your quilting stitches be? In the old days, good quilters sometimes made twelve or thirteen stitches to the inch! Today, six to eight stitches per inch is pretty good. Any more than that is *very* good! Keeping your stitches straight and even is more important than how long or short they are.

|— — — — — —|
Six stitches per inch

|------------|
Thirteen stitches per inch

If you have a problem with your thread tangling or forming unwanted knots, buy beeswax at a fabric store. Running your quilting thread through beeswax will help to keep it from becoming tangled. If the thread continues to tangle, you may want to try threading your needle with a shorter length of thread.

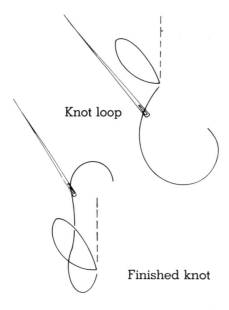

Knot loop

Finished knot

Step 8. When you come to the last 4″ or 5″ of thread in your needle, make a finishing knot this way: Turn your project face down. You will be working with the backing side face up. Run your thread into the backing and bring it out again, making a loop. Do not pull the loop tight! Instead, run your needle and thread through the loop you have just made. This will make a knot. You may want to repeat this process to make a second knot on top of the first one. Then take a long stitch (about 1″), running under the backing fabric and back out. Cut the thread right at the point where it comes out through the backing and the end of the thread will not be noticeable.

Binding the Quilt

Step 1. When all the quilting is done, remove the quilt "sandwich" from the hoop. Take out all the basting stitches.

Step 2. Trim the edges of your "sandwich" evenly all around. Trim right to the edge of the quilt top—so that the excess 2″ or 3″ of batting and backing on all sides is cut away.

Depending on the project you are making, there are two easy ways to finish the ragged edges of your quilt. The following is the easiest method.

Self-binding a Quilt

Step 1. Around the edges of your project, cut away an additional ½″ of batting. This means the top and backing will extend ½″ beyond the newly cut edge of the batting. Do not cut the top or backing fabric while you are trimming this additional ½″ of batting away.

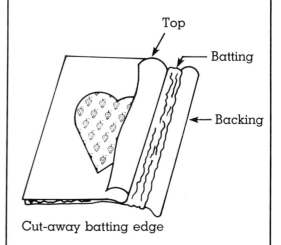

Top

Batting

Backing

Cut-away batting edge

Step 2. On all the outside edges of the backing, fold under the ragged edge about ½" (toward the front of your project). The fold of the backing will now be even with the edge of the batting. Pin the backing edge folded in place. Pin every 2", using straight pins.

Folded backing edge — Fold

Step 3. Next, all the way around the quilt, fold the quilt or project top fabric ½" in (toward the back). As you fold this edge, remove the pin from the folded backing, and re-pin the two folded edges (backing and top) together. The batting now will be hidden inside between the quilt or project top fabric and the backing.

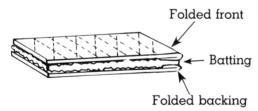

Folded front

← Batting

Folded backing

Folded front edge

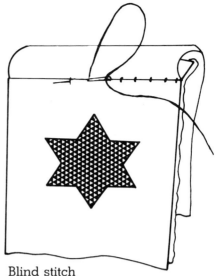

Blind stitch

Step 4. Sew the two folded edges together, using a blind stitch. Use a color of thread that matches your fabric top as nearly as possible. Your needle should come up just in the fold of the top fabric, catch the fold of the backing fabric, and go back in, returning out just in the fold of the top fabric again. This makes the stitching almost invisible. When you have sewn the two folded edges together all the way around your quilt, your project is nearly complete. Now, all you need to do is to stitch or mark your name and the date on it.

Binding with Quilt Binding

Some of the projects call for using quilt binding to finish the edges. This is especially called for in projects that require a "picture frame" effect—like a wall quilt.

Step 1. You will notice that quilt binding has three separate folds. One fold is down the center. In addition, each raw edge of the binding is folded under. (If you cannot find the color of binding that you want, you can use 2″-wide hem facing. Before using it, however, fold it in half with wrong sides together and iron the fold down the center.)

Step 2. Place the quilt so that the front is facing you. Begin in the middle of one side of the quilt. Open the quilt binding and place one edge of it so that it covers about ½″ of the quilt edge. Pin the binding in place all the way to the first corner on your quilt.

Step 3. When you reach the corner, you will have to *miter* or fold the binding so that it looks like the corner on a picture frame. To do this, you will fold under a little triangle of the binding. Pin the mitered corner into place and continue all the way around the quilt edge, mitering each corner as you come to it.

Picture frame corner

Step 4. In pinning the binding, you will end up where you began, and the two ends of the binding will meet. Cover the raw edge of one end of the binding with the folded remaining end of the binding. Pin in place and sew. Cut off any extra binding that is not needed.

Step 5. When one side of the binding is pinned into place all the way around, sew it down, using an appliqué stitch. For an appliqué stitch, use a single strand of knotted thread. Bring the thread up from the underside of the fabric and bring the needle just through the fold in the binding edge (not the fold down the center of the binding). Use thread that matches your binding exactly. Sew the binding into place all the way around the front edge of the quilt. Go back and sew the mitered corners last.

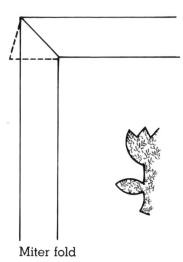

Miter fold

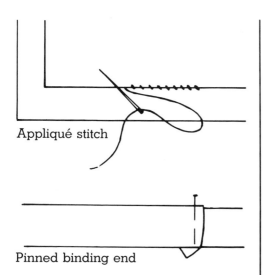

Appliqué stitch

Pinned binding end

Step 6. Turn the quilt over. Pin and sew the binding on the underside of the quilt just as you did on the front. Add your name and the date. Now your project is complete!

The Pieced Potholder

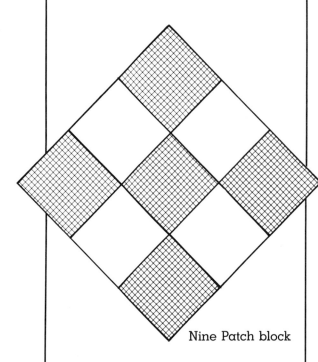

Nine Patch block

Please read chapter "5 About Doing Pieced Work" before beginning this project.

The potholder project offered here is done in the Nine Patch pattern. This is the same pattern that, years ago, many pioneer girls tried for their first quilting project. The Nine Patch is a popular pattern and there are many variations of it. In some variations, a few or all of the squares of the Nine Patch are divided into triangles. Examples of the triangle variations of Nine Patch are found in Project 2, The Pieced Pillow. Perhaps when you finish the potholder, you will want to try this related project.

Making a potholder is a good way to begin learning to quilt. The potholder includes all of the steps needed to make a real, full-size quilt. Yet, it is easy and quick to finish. You might want to make a pair of potholders to give as a gift. If you are making the potholders for one kitchen in particular, remember to choose colors to go with that kitchen.

Tracing and Cutting

Step 1. There is one template pattern for this project. Using a pencil, trace the template onto tracing paper. You will be tracing both a thin outer line and a thick inner line. The outer line will be the *cutting* line for your fabric shapes. The inner line will be your *sewing* line.

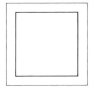

Materials

⅓ yard of fabric A (white muslin)

⅓ yard of fabric B (calico)

One 10″ square of backing fabric (either fabric A or B or a coordinating fabric)

One 3-yard package quilt binding

One 10″ square of polyester batting

One metal ring

Quilting thread

Tools

Tracing paper

Fine sandpaper

Pencil

Scissors

Ruler

Regular sewing thread

Needles (sharps and betweens)

Straight pins

Paper

One small embroidery hoop (4″ to 6″ diameter)

Step 2. Turn over the tracing paper and lay it on the smooth side of a piece of fine sandpaper. Draw over the pattern lines that show through the wrong side of the tracing paper. The pattern will be transferred to the sandpaper below.

Step 3. Take away the tracing paper and darken your pattern lines so that they are easy to see.

Step 4. With scissors, cut out the sandpaper template along the *outer* lines you have drawn.

Step 5. For each fabric you will be working with, place the fabric *right side down* on a flat surface. Use your sandpaper template sand side down (or cardboard template right side down) to trace the *cutting* line for the following:

> 4 squares of fabric A
> 5 squares of fabric B

Step 6. Re-cut your template along the inner line. Your new, re-cut template will now be ¼″ smaller all the way around. Center it exactly on each fabric square that you have traced. Trace around the outside of the new template to mark your *sewing* line on each fabric square.

Step 7. All of your fabric squares now have two lines around them. Cut out each fabric square on the outer *cutting* line, leaving the inner line as a sewing guide.

Sewing the Design

Step 1. Iron all of your fabric squares. Lay them out on a flat surface to form the block.

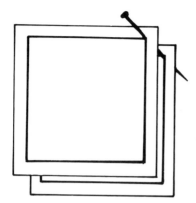

Step 2. You will be using a running stitch to sew each line of three squares into a row. To pin the first two squares together, line up the squares, *right sides together.* Run your pin through the sewing line of the square facing you. Be sure it comes out through the sewing line of the square facing away from you. If the pin is off the sewing line on the square facing away from you, adjust the position of the two squares in relation to each other. Do this at two or three points along the sewing line.

When you are sure the sewing lines of the two squares are lined up exactly, pin the squares together and sew them along one edge. Add the third square for the row by pinning and sewing just as you did the first two squares. Do this for all three rows of fabric squares. As each row is finished, lay it back into place on your flat work surface.

Step 3. Matching seams together, pin the top row of sewn squares to the middle row, *right sides together.* As before, run your pin through the sewing line of the square on one side and be sure it comes out through the sewing line of the square on the other side. Sew the rows together, using a running stitch. When these two rows are joined, pin the last row into place and sew it just as you did the other two. When this is done, your pieced potholder top is complete.

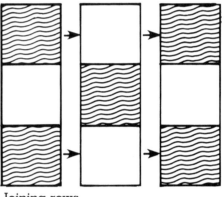

Joining rows

Quilting the Project

Step 1. If you have not already done so, take a moment to read "6 Quilting Makes the Quilt."

Step 2. Iron the Nine Patch block you have sewn. Do not iron the seams open as you would in making clothing. Press seam allowances the same direction. Iron light-colored seams toward dark-colored squares.

Step 3. On a flat surface, place the 10" backing fabric square *right side down.* Put the 10" square of batting on top of the backing square. Place the pressed, Nine Patch block on top of these, *right side up,* and center it carefully. The batting and backing fabric should extend evenly beyond the Nine Patch block all the way around.

Step 4. Pin the potholder "sandwich" of Nine Patch square, batting, and backing in four or five places. Use a contrasting color of thread to baste the layers. Take long basting stitches—about 2" each.

Step 5. You will notice that the heart quilting template for this project has only one outline. Trace the heart quilting template onto tracing paper, transfer it to plain paper, and cut it out. You will use this heart template to guide you as you sew the quilting stitches.

Step 6. Put the potholder "sandwich" into an embroidery hoop. (It is too small for a quilting hoop.) To do this, loosen the larger of the two embroidery hoop circles. Put the smaller hoop on your flat work surface. Place the potholder over the smaller circle and center it. Fit the larger hoop onto the smaller one, stretching the potholder "sandwich" taut and flat between the two hoops. The center square of the potholder should be in the part that is held flat by the hoop. You begin quilting this square first.

Step 7. Pin the paper heart template to the center square. Using a betweens quilting needle and heavy quilting thread, take tiny stitches around the outside of the heart template. When you have finished quilting one heart, unpin the heart template, re-pin it on a new square, and continue quilting. Reposition the potholder in the embroidery hoop as needed. You may find it is easier to do some of the quilting

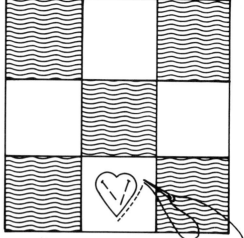

Pinned quilting template

Piecing and quilting diagram

without the hoop. If so, just hold the potholder as flat as possible with your other hand while you quilt. *Do Not Quilt* right to the edge of your project. Leave 1" unquilted all the way around the outside edge.

Step 8. When all the squares are quilted, remove the potholder from the hoop and take out the basting stitches.

Finishing Up

Step 1. Trim away the extra batting and backing fabric to make those layers even with the edges of your potholder top.

Step 2. You will use quilt binding to cover the ragged edge of the potholder. Pin one edge of the binding to the front edge of the potholder all the way around. At each corner, fold a little triangle of the binding under itself to make a diagonal seam. Pin in place. This is called mitering the corners. (Please see "Binding the Quilt" in chapter 6 if you need help.) At the end, cut the binding, making sure to leave one inch extra to hide the cut edges. Turn under, pin, and stitch.

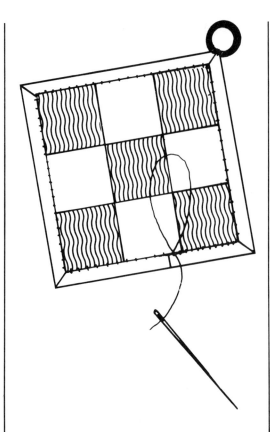

Step 3. Use an appliqué stitch to sew the binding in place on the front of the potholder. Go back and sew the mitered corners.

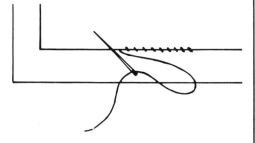

Step 4. Turn the potholder over. Pin and sew the binding on the back just as you did on the front. Attach the metal ring on a corner for hanging.

8

The Pieced Pillow

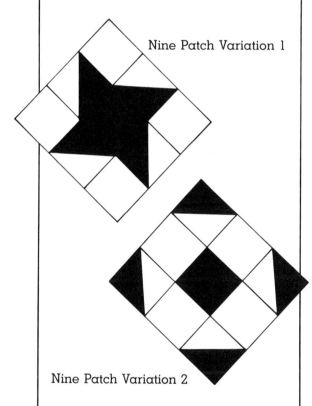

Nine Patch Variation 1

Nine Patch Variation 2

Please read chapter "5 About Doing Pieced Work" before beginning this project.

This pillow project contains variations of the Nine Patch pattern used in Project 1, The Pieced Potholder. In the old days, when a woman chose a pattern for a quilt made for everyday use, she often chose a variation of the Nine Patch. It is a fast, easy pattern and works well with leftover scraps of fabric. Some variations of the basic Nine Patch involve breaking a number of the squares into two triangles each. That is one type of variation that is included in this project.

Before you begin, you will have to decide which variation you want to use for your pillow. One gives you a starlike design in the center. The other two have a checkerboard effect. All three are made from the same combination of squares and triangles. See which one you like best.

If you want to choose your own colors, the best combination might be achieved by using calico for your first fabric (fabric A) and using unbleached muslin for the second fabric (fabric B). Remember, if you are making the pillow as a gift, you may want the colors to match a particular room.

Nine Patch Variation 3

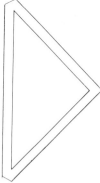

Materials

¼ yard of fabric A (calico)
¾ yard of fabric B (white muslin)
(Two 10" by 15" rectangles will also be cut from this ¾ yard)
One 16" square of batting
One 16" square of pillow top backing fabric (may be any color since it will not show)
One 14" square pillow form

Tools

Tracing paper
Fine sandpaper
Pencil
Masking tape
Scissors
Ruler
Regular sewing thread
Needles (sharps and betweens)
Straight pins
One medium-size embroidery hoop (8" to 10" diameter)
Quilting thread

Tracing and Cutting

Step 1. There are two pattern templates for this project. Using a pencil, trace the templates onto tracing paper. For each, you will be tracing both a thin outer line and a thick inner line. The outer line will be the *cutting* line for your fabric shapes. The inner line will be your *sewing* line.

Step 2. Turn the tracing paper over and lay it on the smooth side of a piece of fine sandpaper. Draw over the pattern lines that show through the wrong side of the tracing paper. The pattern will be transferred to the sandpaper below.

Step 3. Take away the tracing paper and darken your pattern lines.

Step 4. With scissors, cut out the sandpaper templates along the *outer* lines you have drawn.

Step 5. For each fabric you will be working with, place the fabric *right side down* on a flat surface. Use your sandpaper template sand side down (or cardboard template right side down) to trace the *cutting* line for the following:

> 4 triangles of fabric A
> 1 square of fabric A
> 4 triangles of fabric B
> 4 squares of fabric B

Step 6. Re-cut your templates along the inner lines. Your new, re-cut templates should now be ¼" smaller all the way around. Center the square template on each fabric square you have drawn. Trace around the outside of the new template to mark your *sewing* line on each square. Do the same, using the triangle template, for the fabric triangles.

Step 7. All of your fabric squares and triangles now have two lines around them. Cut out each fabric square and triangle on the outer *cutting* line, leaving the inner line as a sewing guide. Reserve the rest of the white muslin (fabric B) for use later.

Sewing the Design

Step 1. Iron all of your fabric shapes. Lay them out on a flat surface to form the pattern variation you have chosen.

Step 2. Begin by sewing each pair of triangles to form a square. To do this, line up the triangles *right sides together*. Run your pin through the sewing lines on either side to make sure the sewing lines of the triangles are lined up exactly. (Review "5 About Doing Pieced Work" if you need help.) Pin the triangles and sew them together. Use the sewing line you have drawn on the fabric as a guide. As each pair of triangles is finished, lay it back into place on your flat work surface.

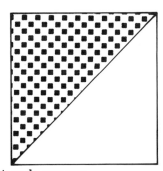

Two-triangle square

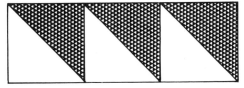

Three-square row

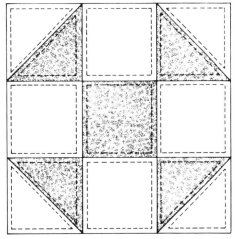

Piecing and quilting diagram

Step 3. Once all the triangles have been sewn together to make squares, join each line of three squares into a row. Pin the pieces you are sewing *right sides together*, using a straight pin to make sure the pieces are lined up correctly. Sew the pieces, using the sewing line you have drawn on the fabric as a guide. As each row is finished, put it back in place on your flat work surface.

Step 4. Matching seams together, sew the three rows of squares together. Use your pin to check that the squares are lined up exactly.

Quilting the Project

Step 1. If you have not already done so, take a moment to read "6 Quilting Makes the Quilt."

Step 2. Iron the Nine Patch variation block you have sewn.

Step 3. On a flat surface, place the pillow top backing fabric square *right side down*. (This square of fabric is the one that will not show, so it may be any color.) On top of this, place the square of batting. Put the pressed Nine Patch block on top of these, right side up, and center it carefully. There should be the same amount of extra batting and pillow top backing fabric sticking out beyond the Nine Patch block all the way around.

Step 4. Pin together the "sandwich" of Nine Patch block, batting, and backing. Use a contrasting color of thread to baste the "sandwich" layers together.

Step 5. Put the "sandwich" into an embroidery hoop. (It is too small for a normal size quilting hoop.) The center square should be held flat by the hoop. You will quilt this part first.

Step 6. Place strips of masking tape directly on your pillow top to guide you in sewing the quilting stitches. The edge of the masking tape should fall about ½" inside each seam on the pillow top.

Step 7. Using a betweens quilting needle and heavy quilting thread, take tiny stitches along the lines you have drawn for quilting the center square. When this is done, quilt the outer squares. You will have to replace the pillow top in the embroidery hoop a number of times. You may find it is easier to do some of the quilting without the hoop. If so, just hold the pillow top as flat as possible in your other hand while you quilt.

Step 8. When all of the squares are quilted, remove the pillow top from the hoop and take out the basting stitches.

Finishing Up

Step 1. If needed, trim the edges of the pillow top slightly to make it even on all four sides.

Step 2. Take the two 10" by 15" rectangles of backing fabric. (These should be cut from fabric B. They will form the fabric back of your pillow.) Put one rectangle of backing fabric on the flat work surface, wrong side up, and so that the longer end goes up and down. Fold one of the long ends under ½" and then ½" again to hide the ragged edge of the fabric underneath. Pin the folded edge in place. Sew the fold down, using a whipstitch. Do the same for the other piece of backing fabric.

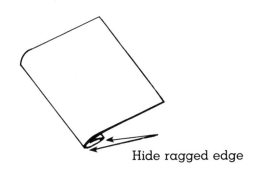

Hide ragged edge

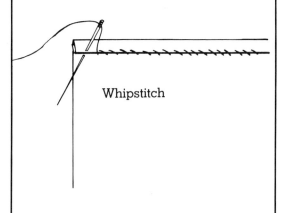

Whipstitch

Step 3. Turn the backing fabric pieces over so that they are right side up. Place the sewn edges one on top of the other so that they overlap by about 2″. Adjust the overlap so that the entire square made by the two backing pieces measures about 15″ on each side. Pin and baste the overlapping pieces in place.

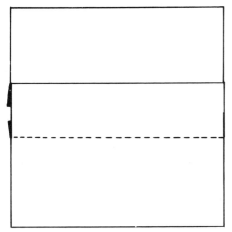

Position backings

Step 4. On the wrong side of the pillow top, mark a sewing line ½″ in all the way around. The line you draw should be 14″ on each side. Do the same for the wrong side of the basted pillow backing.

Step 5. Pin the quilted pillow top and the basted two-piece pillow backing with right sides together. (Run your pin through the sewing lines as you did when piecing the pillow top to be sure the two parts of the pillow are lined up exactly.)

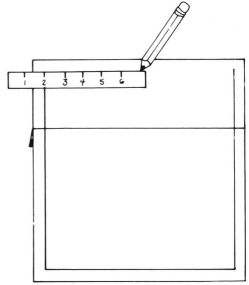

Sewing line

Step 6. Sew the pillow top to the pillow backing on all four sides. Use a running stitch and take a back stitch every five or six stitches. (Or, use a sewing machine.)

Step 7. To finish your pillow and fit it onto the 14″ square pillow form, just remove the basting stitches from the two-piece pillow backing. This will make an opening through which you can fit the pillow form and complete your project.

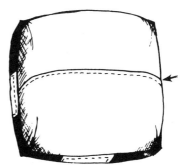

Pillow back opening

The Quilted Gameboard

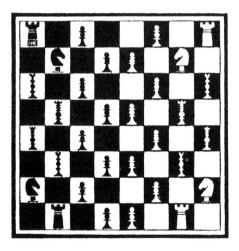

Please read chapter "5 About Doing Pieced Work" before beginning this project.

Ever notice how much a checkerboard or chessboard looks like a little patchwork quilt? You can make a quilted checker or chessboard (they're really the same) for yourself or to give to a friend.

When your checker or chessboard is done, you may want to make a small box or bag for storing it or the game pieces that go with it. You might also find that you are inspired to make other kinds of quilted gameboards. Other games that make good quilted gameboards are Parcheesi and Backgammon.

Decide what you will use for playing pieces before you begin making the gameboard. Otherwise, you may end up with a board whose squares are too big or too small for the checkers or markers you need to play the game.

If you are making a checkerboard, you will need twenty-four checkers—twelve light-colored ones and twelve dark-colored ones. You can use buttons or make checkers from plastic clay that you buy at an art supply store, shape with your hands, and let harden in the oven. Or you might buy real checkers at a toy store, flea market, or tag sale.

If you are making a chessboard, you can make the individual playing pieces out of heavy paper or Bristol board (also available at most art supply stores). Make the playing pieces flat, cut a slit at the bottom, and insert a small piece of paper that runs crossways to make them stand up. You also could use plastic clay to make the pieces or buy real

Materials

½ yard of fabric A (white, pink and green calico)
¼ yard of fabric B (unbleached muslin)
¼ yard of fabric C (rose calico)
¼ yard of fabric D (green calico)
One 18″ square of batting
One 18″ square of backing fabric (may be cut from the ½ yard of fabric A)
One package of ½″ bias tape to match fabric A or fabric B
Thread to match the bias tape exactly
One set of correctly sized playing pieces, or materials to make them
Quilting thread

Tools

Tracing paper
Fine sandpaper
Pencil
Masking tape
Scissors
Ruler
Regular sewing thread
Needles (sharps and betweens)
Straight pins
Paper
One medium-size embroidery hoop (8″ to 10″ diameter)

chess pieces at a toy store or tag sale. In order to use the pattern in this book, be sure your chess pieces are not more than 1½″ across, which is the size of the squares on this gameboard project.

Decide what colors to use in making your gameboard. You can use the colors suggested here. Or you might decide you want to make a traditional gameboard of red and black squares. If you decide to use different colors than those used here, be sure that one is dark and one is light.

Tracing and Cutting

Step 1. There are two pattern templates for this project. Using a pencil, trace the shape of the templates onto tracing paper. You will be tracing both a thin outer line and a thick inner line. The outer line will be the *cutting* line for your fabric shapes. The inner line will be the *sewing* line.

Step 2. Turn the tracing paper over and lay it on the smooth side of a piece of fine sandpaper. Draw over the pattern lines that show through the wrong side of the tracing paper. The pattern will be transferred to the sandpaper below.

Step 3. Take away the tracing paper and darken your pattern lines so they are easy to see.

Step 4. With your scissors, cut out the sandpaper templates along the *outer* pattern lines you have drawn.

Step 5. For each fabric you will be using, place the fabric *right side down* on a flat surface. Use your sandpaper template, sand side down (or cardboard template, right side down) to trace the *cutting* line for the following:

> 32 squares of fabric A
> 32 squares of fabric B
> 36 triangles of fabric C
> 36 triangles of fabric D

Step 6. Re-cut your templates along the inner lines. Your new, re-cut templates should be ¼" smaller all the way around. Center the square template on each fabric square you have already drawn. Trace around the outside of the new template to mark your *sewing* line on each fabric square. Do the same with the triangle template for the fabric triangles.

Step 7. All your fabric squares and triangles now have two lines around them. Cut out each fabric shape on the outer *cutting* line, leaving the inner line as a sewing guide.

Sewing the Design

Step 1. Iron all your fabric shapes. Lay them out on a flat surface to form the pattern. Notice that the light and dark squares *alternate* in the row. Also, if the first row *began* with a *light* square, the second row must *begin* with a *dark* square. This makes your checkerboard pattern.

Step 2. Begin by piecing the squares, then move on to sewing the triangle border separately. Use a running stitch to join each line of eight squares into a row. Begin by pinning two squares together. To do this, line up the squares, *right sides together*, and run your pin through the sewing line of the square facing you. Be sure it comes out through the sewing line of the square facing away from you. If the pin is off the sewing line on the other side, readjust the squares. Do this at two or three points along the sewing line, so you will know if the two squares are lined up exactly. Pin the squares and sew them together. Continue to pin and sew enough squares to make a row of eight squares across. Sew the squares together: one dark, one light, one dark, and so on. As before, use your pin to help you line up the sewing lines of the squares exactly. When you finish the first row of squares, lay it back in place on the flat work surface.

Step 3. Sew the remaining squares into seven more rows like the first one. As you finish each row, lay it back in place on the flat surface. Check to make sure that your light and dark squares *alternate* both across and up and down.

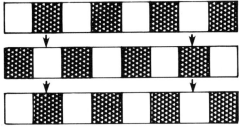
Joining strips of squares

Step 4. Matching seams together, pin the top row of sewn squares to the next row down, right sides together. As before, use your pin to match up the sewing lines. Sew the two rows together, using a running stitch. Sew the remaining rows together in the same way. Join the squares in such a way that two light squares and two dark squares are never next to each other. When all of the squares are sewn together, you will have finished the main part of the gameboard.

Step 5. Now you are ready to begin sewing the border of triangles. With right sides together, pin and sew one dark triangle to one light triangle together on the long sides of the triangles. This will make a two-color square. Sew all the triangles this way to make them into two-color squares. Join the triangles just as you did the earlier squares, using a pin to check that the sewing lines on either side of the triangles are lined up exactly.

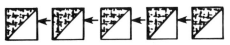
Joining triangles for border

Step 6. When all the two-color (triangle) squares are sewn, sew ten of them into a strip.

Step 7. Sew ten more two-color squares into a strip. Then sew a strip of eight two-color squares and another strip of eight two-color squares.

Step 8. You are now ready to join the triangle border to the main part of the gameboard. You have two long border strips and two short ones. Matching seams as you go, pin and sew one long border strip to one side of the main part of the board.

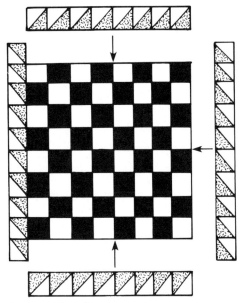
Pinning border strips

Step 9. Pin and sew the other long border strip to the opposite side of the gameboard. Match the seams as you go. Then sew the two short border strips, one on each of the remaining sides. Join the strips at each corner, and you've finished piecing your gameboard!

Quilting the Project

Step 1. If you have not already done so, take a moment to read chapter "6 Quilting Makes the Quilt." Then iron the pieced gameboard you have sewn.

Step 2. On your flat work surface, place the backing fabric square right side *down*. On top of this, place the square of batting. Put the ironed, pieced gameboard on top of these, right side *up*, and center it carefully. Be sure that the batting and backing stick out the same amount beyond the gameboard all the way around.

Step 3. Pin together a "sandwich" of the pieced gameboard, batting, and backing fabric in four or five places. Use a contrasting color of thread to baste the three "sandwich" layers together.

Step 4. There are two quilting templates for this project—the heart and the square. You will notice that they each have only one outline. Trace the quilting templates onto tracing paper and transfer them to plain paper. Then cut them out.

Step 5. Decide which color square on your gameboard is to be quilted with a heart and which will be quilted with a square. (In our example, the solid color squares are quilted with a heart. The print squares are quilted in a square shape.) Then pin the heart pattern in place on a square near the center. You will want to quilt from the center out.

Step 6. Put the gameboard "sandwich" into an embroidery hoop. The center of the "sandwich" is the part that should be held flat by the hoop—and that you will quilt first. Using a betweens needle and heavy quilting thread, take tiny stitches around the outside of the heart template. When you have completed a line of quilting around one heart, you've finished quilting one whole gameboard square.

Step 7. Unpin the heart pattern, re-pin it on the next square in the same color, and quilt. Reposition your gameboard in the embroidery hoop as needed. You may find it is easier to do some quilting without the hoop. If so, just hold the gameboard flat with your other hand as you quilt.

Step 8. When all the gameboard squares that need quilted hearts are done, quilt the remaining gameboard squares, using the square quilting template.

Step 9. Try quilting the triangle border freehand. Or stick small strips of masking tape directly on the project to use as a guide for quilting straight lines. The edge of the masking tape should fall about ⅛" inside the triangles nearest the gameboard squares. Follow this line, quilting all the way around the outside of the board until you are back to where you began. Then quilt just inside the outer triangles all the way around, using the same method. When all the quilting is done, remove the basting stitches.

Finishing Up

Step 1. Trim away the excess batting and backing fabric from your project.

Step 2. We used a self bias binding in our photographed example, but you will use a readymade bias tape to cover the ragged edge of the gameboard, just as you would use quilt binding to cover the rough edges of a real quilt. Pin one edge of the bias tape to the front edge of your

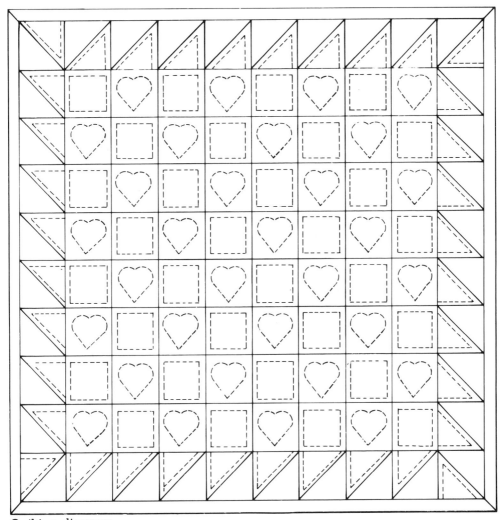

Quilting diagram

gameboard all the way around. As you come to each corner, fold the tape so that it makes a little triangle of fabric under itself. This will make a diagonal seam show at the corner—like on a picture frame. This is called *mitering* the corner. (Please review "Binding the Quilt" from chapter "6 Quilting Makes the Quilt" if you need help.) Pin each mitered corner as you go. When you have pinned the bias tape on all four sides, leave about 3" of extra tape at the end, and cut off the remainder.

Step 3. Using hidden appliqué stitches, sew the bias tape to the top of the quilt edge all the way around. Go back and sew each mitered corner separately.

Step 4. Pin the other edge of the bias tape to the back of the gameboard and sew it in place. To finish, cut the excess tape so there is only about ½" extra. Turn under ¼" of this and stitch down the end of the bias tape to complete your project.

Amish Mini Quilt

Please read chapter "5 About Doing Pieced Work" before beginning this project.

Many quilt collectors like Amish quilts because they remind them of modern art paintings. They have strong, simple shapes and rich, solid colors. You can make a miniature Amish quilt just like the large ones that are so prized by quilt collectors today.

The Bars pattern has always been popular among traditional Amish quilters. It is a simple pattern. On large quilts, it gives its maker a chance to show off her fanciest quilting stitches. Traditionally, those quilting stitches were done, not in white thread as with most quilts, but in black or navy blue thread. Fortunately, you should have no trouble finding colored quilting thread at a fabric store.

Tracing and Cutting

Step 1. There are three template patterns for this project. Using a pencil, trace the shape of each template onto tracing paper. For all, you will be tracing both a thin outer line and a thick inner line. The *outer* line will be your *cutting* line. The inner line will be your *sewing* line.

Materials

⅓ yard of fabric A (dark green)
⅓ yard of fabric B (maroon)
⅓ yard of fabric C (dusty rose)
18″ square of batting
18″ square of backing fabric (may be any dark, solid color)
Black or navy blue quilting thread

Tools

Tracing paper
Fine sandpaper
Pencil
Masking tape
Scissors
Ruler
Regular sewing thread
Needles (sharps and betweens)
Straight pins
One pair of small quilting hoops (14″ diameter)

Step 2. Turn over the tracing paper and lay it on the smooth side of a piece of fine sandpaper. Draw over the pattern lines that show through the wrong side of the tracing paper. The pattern will rub off onto the sandpaper below.

Step 3. Take away the tracing paper and darken your pattern lines.

Step 4. With scissors, cut out the sandpaper templates along the *outer* lines you have drawn.

Step 5. For each fabric, place the fabric *right side down* on a flat surface. Use your sandpaper template sand side down (or cardboard template right side down) to trace the *cutting* line for the following:

> 4 squares of fabric A (dark green)
> 2 narrow rectangles fabric A (dark green)
> 4 wide rectangles fabric B (maroon)
> 3 narrow rectangles fabric C (dusty rose)

Step 6. After you have marked all the pieces, re-cut your templates along the inner lines. Your new, re-cut templates should be ¼″ smaller than they were all the way around. Center the square template exactly on each fabric square you have drawn. Trace around the outside of the new template to mark your *sewing* line on each square. Do the same with each of the remaining templates and fabric rectangles.

Step 7. All of your fabric squares and rectangles now have two lines around them. Cut out each fabric shape on the outer *cutting* line, leaving the inner line as a sewing guide.

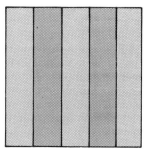

Five rectangles joined

Sewing the Design

Step 1. Iron all the fabric shapes. Lay them out on your flat work surface to form the pattern.

Step 2. Begin by sewing the five narrow rectangles together. To do this, line up the first two rectangles, right sides together. Run your pin through the sewing lines on either side to be sure the rectangles are lined up correctly. (Please review chapter "5 About Doing Pieced Work" if you need help.) Pin the rectangles right sides together and sew them along one long side. Use the sewing line you have drawn as a guide. When the first two rectangles have been sewn together, go on and add the remaining rectangles to form the center bars of the pattern. When all the bars have been joined, lay them back on your work surface so you know that you are sewing your pattern pieces in the right order.

Step 3. Next, sew the first wide rectangle lengthwise across the top of the center bars. Sew the second wide rectangle lengthwise across the bottom of the center bars. Add the remaining wide rectangles, one on either side of the bars. Remember to pin the pieces right sides together before sewing and to use your pin to help you line up the sewing lines.

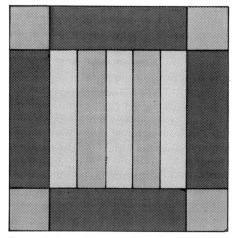

Remaining pieces joined

Step 4. Pin and sew each square, first to one wide rectangle end, then to the other until all four squares are sewn in place. Be sure the seams match up with one another.

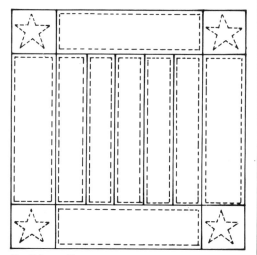

Quilting diagram

Quilting the Project

Step 1. If you have not already done so, take a minute to read "6 Quilting Makes the Quilt."

Step 2. Iron the Amish Bars mini quilt top you have sewn.

Step 3. On a flat surface, place the backing fabric square *right side down*. On top of this, place the square of batting. Put the ironed mini quilt top on top of these, *right side up,* and center it in place. There should be the same amount of extra batting and backing fabric sticking out all the way around.

Step 4. Pin together the "sandwich" of mini quilt top, batting, and backing fabric. Use a contrasting color of thread to baste the three "sandwich" layers together.

Step 5. There is one quilting template for this project. You will notice that it has only one outline. Trace the star quilting template for this project onto tracing paper and transfer it to a piece of plain paper. Then cut it out. This template is for the quilting that goes in the four corner squares.

Step 6. Put the mini quilt "sandwich" into the quilting hoop. The center of the design should be the part that is held flat by the hoop. You will begin to quilt this area first.

Step 7. Put strips of masking tape directly onto your project to use as a guide in helping you to stitch straight lines of quilting. The edge of the masking tape should fall ¼" inside each rectangle.

Step 8. Using a betweens quilting needle and a single, knotted strand of heavy black or navy blue quilting thread, take tiny stitches along the edges of the masking tape you have placed on the center bars. Then go on to quilt the outer rectangles. You will have to reposition the "sandwich" in the hoop a number of times. You may find it easier to do some of the quilting without the hoop. If so, just hold the mini quilt "sandwich" as flat as possible in your other hand while you quilt. *Do not quilt* right to the edge of your project. Leave 1" unquilted all the way around the outer edge.

Step 9. To quilt the corner squares, pin the paper template in place and sew around it. Re-pin it in each of the remaining corners as you go.

Step 10. When all the quilting is done, remove the mini quilt "sandwich" from the hoop and take out the basting stitches.

Finishing Up

Step 1. Trim away the extra batting and backing fabric to make them even with the edges of your quilt top. Then, all the way around, cut away the batting by an additional ½". Do not cut the backing or the top of your project.

Step 2. All the way around your project, fold and pin the backing fabric ½" in (toward the front) so the fold in the backing meets the edge of the batting.

Step 3. Next, all the way around, fold the top ½" in (toward the back). As you fold this edge, remove the folded backing pins and re-pin the two folded edges (backing and top) together, hiding the batting edge inside.

Step 4. Using a blind stitch, sew the folded edges together all the way around the quilt. Let the thread come out just in the fold of the quilt top and go in just in the fold of the backing—so that the stitching is almost invisible. When all four edges of the quilt are sewn and you have added your name and the date, your mini quilt will be completed.

Square Within a Square Wall Hanging

The pattern that makes up the main part of this wall hanging is called Square Within a Square. It is an old, traditional pattern with many variations. It is a good pattern for so-called "scrap" quilts—quilts made from leftover fabric. In early days, the fabric pieces left over from a woman's household sewing sometimes were small. Even these small pieces of fabric were saved to make scrap quilts.

The pieced outer border of the wall hanging is a pattern known as Flying Geese. Generations ago, New England colonists looked up at the sky and saw long lines of Canadian geese flying overhead in "V" formation. They translated this image into the lines of triangles that form the Flying Geese pattern. Sometimes Flying Geese is used as a border, as it is here. Sometimes strips of triangles are put between solid bands of fabric to make an entire quilt in the Flying Geese pattern.

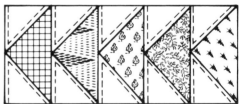

Flying Geese pattern

Please read chapter "5 About Doing Pieced Work" before beginning this project.

The sample for this project has been made as a scrap quilt. It contains nine different blue calicoes and nine green calicoes. Each block for this project has three squares: a white center square, a blue middle square, and a green-and-white outer square. In deciding on your own color combination, you may want to use only two colors of calico throughout. This means you would use white muslin for the inner squares, one calico for all the middle squares, and another calico plus white for all the outer squares.

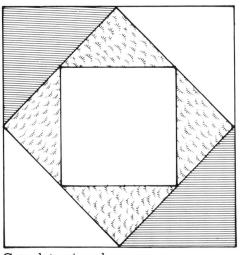

Complete pieced square

Materials

Nine ¼-yard scraps of blue calicoes
Nine ¼-yard scraps of green calicoes
1 yard of white muslin
One 36″ square of batting
One 36″ square of white muslin backing fabric
Four packages of green calico ¾″ bias tape
Regular sewing thread to match the bias tape exactly
Quilting thread

Tools

Tracing paper
Fine sandpaper
Pencil
Masking tape
Scissors
Ruler
Regular sewing thread
Needles (sharps and betweens)
Straight pins
One pair of 14″ quilting hoops

If you decide to make a "scrap" quilt wall hanging similar to the one pictured, you will use nine kinds of one color of calico (nine different blues, for instance) for the middle squares. Then use nine kinds of a different color calico (nine greens, for example) for the outer squares. Use alternating colors for the triangle border. If you are making the wall hanging for a certain room, be sure to choose colors that look nice with the colors that are already in the room.

You should feel free to choose your own colors to work with for this project. However, the colors used in the photograph of this wall hanging will be given in the project directions to make them easier to understand. If you are using colors different from those suggested, you might want to begin by pencilling in your own colors above the colors named in the directions.

Note: Fabric stores often sell pre-cut quarter yards of calico for quilts and craft projects. Or your family members and friends who sew may have fabric to share with you.

Tracing and Cutting

Step 1. There are five fabric templates for this project. Using a pencil, trace the shape of the templates onto tracing paper. For each, you will be tracing both a thin outer line and a thick inner line. The outer line will be the *cutting* line for your fabric shapes. The inner line will be your *sewing* line.

Step 2. Turn the tracing paper over and lay it on the smooth side of a piece of fine sandpaper. Draw over the pattern lines that show through the wrong side of the tracing paper. The pattern will rub off onto the sandpaper below.

Step 3. Take away the tracing paper and darken your pattern lines so they are easy to see.

Step 4. With scissors, cut the sandpaper templates along the *outer* line you have drawn.

Step 5. For each fabric, place the fabric on a work surface *right side down.* Use your sandpaper template sand side down (or cardboard template right side down) to trace the *cutting* lines for the following:

> Eighteen large green triangles (two of each kind of green calico)
>
> Eighteen large white triangles
>
> Thirty-six medium blue triangles (four of each kind of blue calico
>
> Nine large white squares for the main blocks and four small white squares for the corner blocks
>
> Thirty-six large blue border triangles (four of each kind of blue calico)
>
> Thirty-six large green border triangles (four of each kind of green calico)
>
> 144 small white border triangles

Step 6. After marking all of the pieces, re-cut the large triangle template along the inner line. Your new, re-cut template should be ¼″ smaller all the way around. Center this smaller template on each of the large triangle fabric shapes that you originally drew. Trace around the outside of the new template to mark your *sewing* line on each of the fabric triangles.

Step 7. Re-cut the rest of the templates and trace the sewing lines on the rest of the fabric shapes, just as you did for the large triangles.

Step 8. All your fabric triangles and squares now have two lines around them. Cut out each fabric triangle and square on the outer *cutting* line, leaving the inner line as a sewing guide.

Sewing the Design

Step 1. Iron all fabric triangles and squares. Lay out the fabric shapes to make the first block.

Step 2. You will be sewing the Square Within a Square part of the pattern first. This consists of nine separate blocks. You will sew each block completely before going on to the next block. Then, when all the blocks are done, you will go on to sew the Flying Geese borders. Before you start sewing, however, organize all your triangles into piles so that the different colors of blue and green calicoes will not get mixed up from block to block.

Step 3. Lay out the shapes for the first block in the order they are to appear when finished. To begin sewing the first block, hold one of the four medium-size blue triangles upright. The longest side, or base, of the triangle should be at the bottom. Using a running stitch, and with right sides together, sew this base to one side of the first white square. Then sew the remaining three blue triangles for this block on the remaining three sides of the white square. (Remember to use your pin to help line up the sewing lines of the fabric shapes, or see "5 About Doing Pieced Work" for help.) When all four blue triangles are sewn in place, you will have a new, larger square.

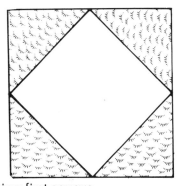

Piecing first square

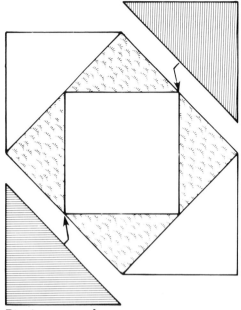

Piecing second square

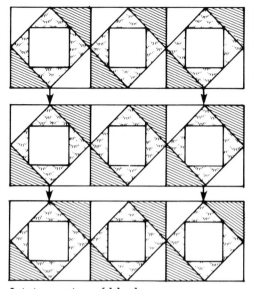

Joining strips of blocks

Step 4. On the four sides of the new square, sew two large green calico triangles (by their bases) on opposite sides of the new square. Then sew two large white triangles on the remaining sides of the square. This completes your first block.

Step 5. Lay out and sew the remaining eight blocks just as you did for the first block. When all the blocks are pieced, iron them carefully.

Step 6. Lay out the nine completed blocks in the order you want them to appear in your finished wall quilt. Matching seams together, pin and sew the blocks into three separate rows of three blocks each. Then sew the three rows to make a large square of nine blocks. (Remember to pin right sides together and to use your pin to be sure the sewing lines are lined up. See "5 About Doing Pieced Work" for help.)

Step 7. Open one package of the bias tape. Pin one edge of the bias tape ¼" in all the way around the ragged edges of the large nine-block square. Use a blind (or appliqué) stitch to sew the bias tape onto the nine-block square. As you come to each corner, make a fold in the bias tape to "miter" the corner. It will look a little like the corner on a picture frame. (If you need help, please see "Binding the Quilt" from chapter "6 Quilting Makes the Quilt.")

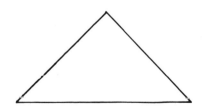

Triangle upright showing base

Step 8. To begin piecing the border of the wall hanging, hold the first calico triangle upright. Sew the base of one white triangle to the right side of the calico triangle. Then sew the base of another white triangle to the left side of the calico triangle. This will make a pieced rectangle. (Remember to pin the sides being sewn right sides together and to use your pin to line up the sewing lines or see "5 About Doing Pieced Work" for help.) Do the same for all of the calico border triangles to make 72 pieced rectangles.

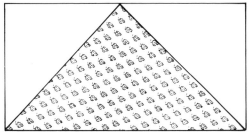

Triangle/rectangle

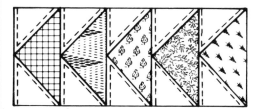

Flying Geese quilting diagram

Step 9. Sew the pieced rectangles together in long strips to make the borders. Alternate the colored rectangles—that is, sew one blue, one green, one blue, and so on. Allow eighteen rectangles for each border strip. To sew the first two rectangles together, fold the first rectangle in half. On the wrong side of the fabric, make a dot with your pencil on the base of the triangle right where the fold is. With right sides together, line up this dot with the point of the triangle in the next rectangle. Line up the

sewing lines with the help of your pin, then pin and sew the two rectangles together. Do this for the rest of the triangles in the four border strips.

Step 10. Pin and sew the bias tape edge of the large nine-block square to the border strips. Pin the tape on top of the edge of each border strip and use a blind stitch to sew it in place. Be sure to have the bias tape meet exactly at the end of each calico border triangle. In addition, match the seams of each border strip with the seams of the nine-block square where the triangle points meet.

Step 11. With right sides together, pin and sew the four white corner squares to the rest of the border. Let the mitered corners of the bias tape overlap the border squares slightly. To finish, pin and sew the mitered corners of the bias tape in place, using a blind stitch.

Quilting the Project

Step 1. If you have not already done so, take a moment to read "6 Quilting Makes the Quilt."

Step 2. Iron the pieced Square Within a Square wall quilt top you have sewn.

Step 3. On a flat surface, lay the backing fabric *right side down*. On top of this, place the square of batting. Place the ironed Square Within a Square quilt top on these *right side up* and center it. This makes a "sandwich" of backing fabric, batting, and quilt top. There should be the same amount of extra batting and backing fabric sticking out beyond the pieced wall quilt top all the way around.

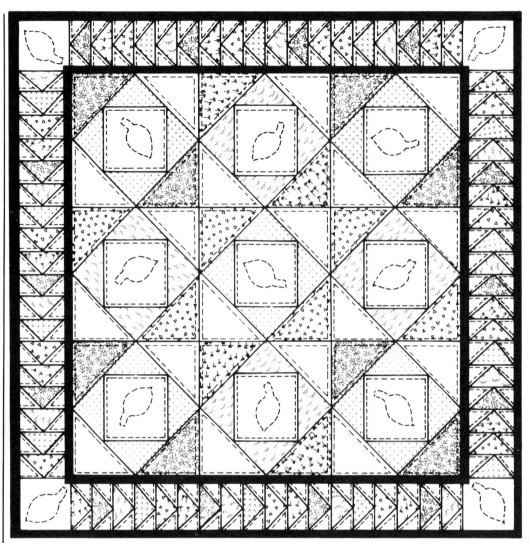

Wall hanging piecing
and quilting diagram

Quilting diagram of single block

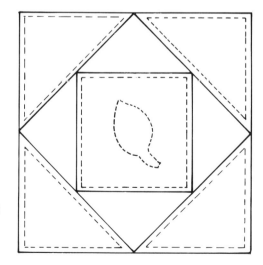

Step 4. Pin together the "sandwich" of pieced Square Within a Square, batting, and backing. Use a contrasting color of thread to baste the layers together. Take long basting stitches—about 2" long.

Step 5. Using a pencil and tracing paper, trace the quilting template for the white center squares and the four white border corners onto plain white paper.

Step 6. Put the center block of the wall quilt into the quilting hoop. When it is taut, put a strip of masking tape directly on your wall quilt top to use as a guideline for making straight lines of quilting stitches. The masking tape should be about ¼" inside each seam on the triangles for the Square Within a Square pattern. You will be able to pick up and replace the masking tape as you stitch more lines of quilting. For the Flying Geese border, you will want to use the masking tape to mark about ¼" outside the calico triangles.

Step 7. Use a betweens quilting needle and one strand of heavy quilting thread knotted at the end. Take tiny stitches along the masking tape for the center block. When the lines of quilting are complete, pin the paper quilting template in place on the white inner square. Quilt all around the outside of the quilting template.

Step 8. Remove the hoop from the wall quilt and place it on a new block. Quilt the rest of the blocks just as you did the center one.

Step 9. You may find it easier to quilt the border without the hoop. If so, hold the edge of the "sandwich" as flat as possible in your other hand as you quilt. Quilt ¼" around the outside of each triangle. When you have finished quilting, take out the basting stitches.

Finishing Up

Step 1. Trim the extra batting and backing fabric so that they are the same as your quilt top.

Step 2. Open the remaining packages of bias tape. Turn the "sandwich" over so the quilted top is facing *down*. Pin the tape ½" in and all the way around the outside edge of the "sandwich." Miter each corner as you come to it. (See "Binding the Quilt" from "6 Quilting Makes the Quilt" if you need help.) When you come to the end of the first package of tape, cover the ragged end with the folded-under beginning of the tape from the second package. Use a blind stitch to sew the tape in place.

Step 3. Turn the "sandwich" over so the right side is facing you. Pin the bias tape ½" in all around the ragged edge of the top (just as you did the back) and sew in place. Did you remember to add your name and the date? If not, now is the time to do so.

Step 4. To hang your wall quilt, you may want to make four loops from the extra bias tape. Cut four 4" strips of bias tape. Fold them in half and sew them to the top from the back of the hanging. As you sew, fold under the ragged edge of each loop you have made. Through the loops, insert a wooden dowel rod (you can get them at almost any hardware store) and your Square Within a Square wall quilt will be ready to be displayed.

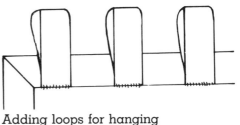

Adding loops for hanging

Pieced Single Bed Quilt

Please read chapter "5 About Doing Pieced Work" before beginning this project.

Picture yourself stepping out of a frontier cabin one morning and finding the footprint of a bear in the ground outside your doorstep. Would you have been frightened or pleased to know that you had had such a visitor during the night? Today people seldom see bears in the wild. Many kinds of bears are threatened or, like the grizzly, in danger of becoming extinct.

The Bear's Paw is the name of the quilt pattern for this project. It is an old pattern that was especially popular during frontier days. It took on this name in areas where pioneers saw bears in the wilderness. In more settled areas, the same pattern took on a different name to match the surroundings. Duck's Foot in the Mud is one example. In another part of the country—among the Quakers of Pennsylvania—the same pattern was called Hand of Friendship.

The Bear's Paw quilt offered here is for a single bed. When you finish it and the other pieced projects in this book, you will have worked with all of the basic geometric shapes used in straight pieced work—the triangle, square, rectangle, and diamond!

This is a much larger and more challenging project than the others in this book. Perhaps you would enjoy having a special project for you and your mother to work on together. If so, this would be a good

one to try. Making quilts together brings people closer. It also makes the quilt finish up faster! Maybe you and your mother could complete this as a joint project in honor of an important event in your life—your graduation, for instance. In the old days, when a girl went out into the world on her own, she proudly took along the quilts she had made. Think how proud you will feel one day, setting up your own room or apartment with the quilt you have made yourself. Some things never change.

Although you are encouraged to use your own color combination, the colors white, green, and red will be used in the directions for this project to make the directions easier to understand. But feel free to choose your own colors. If you do, you might want to begin by writing in pencil the colors you have chosen above the colors named in the directions.

Traditionally, the white areas in this design are always white, but you may wish to substitute a solid color and/or use two colorful calicoes for the rest of the pattern. The large white squares of this pattern were often quilted with a fancy design known as the Princess Feather. In this project, the quilting templates for the large white squares are in the shapes of bears and hearts to show the need to protect bears in the world today!

Materials

6 yards white muslin
2½ yards of green fabric
2½ yards of red fabric
6 yards of 45" wide batting
3 yards 72" or 90" wide
   muslin quilt backing (or
   two 3-yard lengths of 45"
   wide muslin sewn together
   lengthwise)
Four 3-yard packages of quilt
   binding to match one of
   the colored fabrics

Tools

Tracing paper
Fine sandpaper
Pencil
Masking tape
Scissors
Ruler
Regular sewing thread
Needles (sharps and
   betweens quilting)
Straight pins
One pair large quilting hoops
   (24" in diameter)
White quilting thread

Tracing and Cutting

Step 1. There are six pattern templates for this project. Using a pencil, trace the shape of the templates onto tracing paper. For each, you will be tracing both a thin outer line and a thick inner line. The outer line will be your *cutting* line. The inner line will be your *sewing* line.

Step 2. Turn over the tracing paper and place it on the smooth side of a piece of fine sandpaper. Draw over the pattern lines that show through the wrong side of the tracing paper. The pattern will rub off onto the sandpaper below.

Step 3. Take away the tracing paper and darken your pattern lines.

Step 4. With scissors, cut out the sandpaper templates along the *outer* lines you have drawn.

Step 5. For each fabric, place the fabric *right side down* on a flat surface. Use your sandpaper template sand side down (or cardboard template right side down) to trace the *cutting* line for the templates. For each block you will need: 4 white rectangles, 8 small white triangles, 4 small white squares, 1 large green square, 4 large red triangles, 8 red diamonds, and 8 green diamonds. This means that for twenty pieced blocks, you will need to cut out a total of the following pieces:

> 80 white rectangles
> 160 small white triangles
> 80 small white squares
> 20 large green squares
> 80 large red triangles
> 160 red diamonds
> 160 green diamonds

Step 6. After you have marked all the pieces, re-cut your templates along the inner lines. Your new, re-cut templates will be ¼″ smaller all the way around. Center the diamond template on each fabric diamond you have drawn. Trace around the outside of the new template to mark your *sewing* line on each diamond. Do the same for each of the remaining shapes.

Step 7. All your fabric shapes now have two lines around them. Cut out each fabric shape on the outer *cutting* line, leaving the inner line as a sewing guide.

Step 8. From the remaining white fabric, measure and mark twenty large, white 12½″ squares. (You may want to make your own template for these large squares.) All the way around each square, measure and mark a line ¼" in from the first line you drew. The outer line will be your *cutting* line for the large squares. The inner line will be your *sewing* line.

Step 9. Cut out the twenty large white squares on the outer *cutting* lines and set them aside.

Sewing the Design

Step 1. Iron all your fabric shapes. Lay out enough shapes in the form of the first pieced block you will sew.

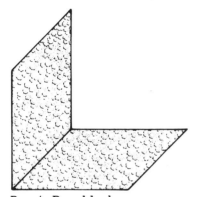

Piecing Bear's Paw block

Step 2. You will want to sew each pieced block completely before going on to the next block. Think of each block as four connected mini squares. Each mini square is one bear's "paw." To start, you will be sewing together the pieces to make each of the four "paw" mini squares for the first block. Begin by sewing together one pair of red diamonds along one long side. To do this, line up the diamonds with right sides together. Run your pin through the sewing lines on either side to be sure the diamonds are lined up correctly. (Please see "5 About Doing Pieced Work" if you need help.) Pin the diamonds with right sides together and sew them along one long side. When

these are sewn, sew the remaining three pairs of red diamonds just as you did the first pair.

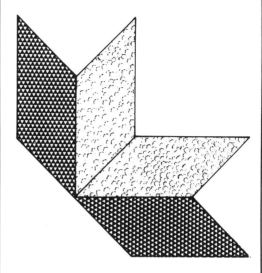

Step 3. To each pair of red diamonds add a green diamond on either side. Remember to pin the diamonds *right sides together* and to use your pin to help you line up the sewing lines.

Step 4. Next, for each of the four "paw" mini squares, you will fill in the spaces between the points of the diamonds and at the base of the "paw." This will make four small pieced squares. Between each green and red diamond point, sew a small white triangle. Between the two red diamond points, sew a small white square. At the base of each "paw," sew a large red triangle. Remember to pin and line up the fabric shapes with *right sides together*. Use a pin to help you line up the sewing lines. Sew one side of each triangle or square at a time.

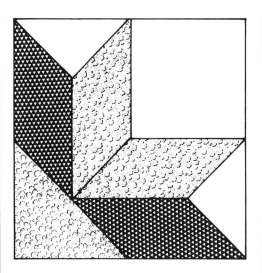

Step 5. Sew a white rectangle between two bear's "paw" mini squares. Lay the joined pair of "paws" back down on your work surface on the correct side of the block where they will finally appear. Do the same for the remaining pair of "paws."

Complete Bear's Paw block

Step 6. Sew a long strip made from one remaining white rectangle, one green square, and a last white rectangle. Matching seams together, join the two pairs of "paws" with the rectangular strip in-between. This will complete your first Bear's Paw block.

Step 7. Sew the remaining nineteen pieced Bear's Paw blocks (there are twenty in all) just as you did the first one.

Setting the Quilt

Setting a quilt simply means "sewing all of the blocks together." If you were to sew blocks together in rows, it would be more difficult to line the seams up properly. Your seams might not come together perfectly and that would not look nice. Instead, you will be joining your blocks in groups of four blocks or six blocks each. Then you will sew these groups of blocks together. As you work, be sure to pay careful attention to matching seams! Pin the blocks or groups of blocks with *right sides together* and check them one last time from the right side before sewing them in place.

Step 1. Organize your blocks so that you have a pile of pieced blocks and one of plain blocks.

Step 2. With *right sides together*, pin the first pieced block and the first plain block along one side. Use your pin to help line up the sewing lines. Sew the two blocks together.

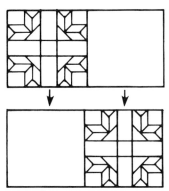

Joining blocks

Step 3. Sew two more blocks together the same way. Now sew these two *pairs* of blocks together to make a square of four blocks. Be sure to alternate pieced and plain blocks. Sew a total of thirty-two blocks (eighteen pieced and eighteen plain) into squares of four blocks each. This will give you eight 4-block squares.

Step 4. Set aside four of the eight 4-block squares. Join one pieced and one plain block to this square along one side. Now you will have a rectangle of six blocks. Do the same for the other three 4-block squares that you set aside.

Step 5. You now have four 4-block squares and four 6-block rectangles. Lay them out as they will appear when the quilt is finished. Join one 4-block square to one 6-block rectangle. Add on the next four-block square to the large ten-block group you have just sewn. Join to it the next six-block rectangle and continue adding on four-block squares and six-block rectangles to complete the quilt top.

Quilting the Project

Step 1. Please take a moment to read "6 Quilting Makes the Quilt" before going on with this project.

Step 2. Iron the Bear's Paw quilt top you have pieced.

Step 3. On a large, flat surface (perhaps a clean swept floor), place the backing fabric *right side down*. If you are using 90″ wide muslin backing, you are all ready. If you are using two 3-yard lengths of backing fabric, these will first have to be sewn together lengthwise—preferably on a sewing machine.

Step 4. Cut the batting so that you have two 90″ lengths of batting. Place the two lengths of batting side by side on top of the backing fabric, overlapping them in the middle about 2″.

Step 5. Put the ironed quilt top *right side up* on top of these. There should be about the same amount of extra batting and backing fabric sticking out all the way around. Trim the excess batting and backing fabric so that they extend about 3″ beyond the quilt top on each side.

Step 6. Pin together the "sandwich" of quilt top, batting, and backing fabric. Pin about every 12″.

Step 7. When the entire quilt "sandwich" is pinned, baste the "sandwich" together, using a contrasting color of thread and taking long, 2″ to 3″ basting stitches. Run a line of basting down the middle from top to bottom. Run another line of basting across the middle from side to side. Run a third from the upper right corner to the lower left corner. Let a fourth run from the upper left corner to the lower right corner. Fill in with extra lines of basting stitches so that no area larger than 12″ square is left unbasted.

Twin-size bed quilt piecing and quilting diagram

Step 8. Cut out the bear and heart quilting templates for this project and set them aside. (Notice that these templates have only one outline each.)

Step 9. Put the center area of your quilt "sandwich" into the quilting hoop. This center area should be held fairly taut by the hoop. You will be quilting from the center of the quilt outward, so this center area should be quilted first.

Step 10. For plain blocks, use the bear and heart templates as quilting guides. Pin the paper templates in place and quilt around the outside of them. Remove and re-pin the templates as needed. For pieced blocks, put strips of masking tape on your quilt top to use as a guide for sewing straight lines of quilting. You can quilt right along the edge of the masking tape. Run the quilting ¼" around the inside of the green square and ¼" around the outside of each "paw" on the pieced blocks.

Step 11. When the center area is quilted, remove the "sandwich" from the hoop. Reposition the hoop so that the area just outside the center is held taut by the hoop. Continue quilting. Replace the "sandwich" as needed in the hoop. Always quilt from the "inside" toward the "outside" edges. *Do not quilt* to the outer edges of the quilt. Leave about 1" unquilted on all the outside edges of your project.

Finishing Up

Step 1. Trim away the extra batting and backing fabric to make them even with the edges of your quilt top.

Step 2. Pin one edge of the quilt binding along the front of your quilt so as to cover the ragged edge. As you come to each corner, you will "miter" it; that is, you will fold a little triangle of fabric under itself to make a diagonal seam in the corner.

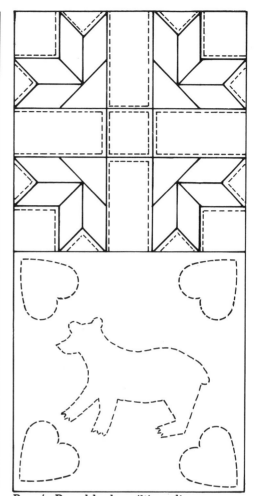

Bear's Paw block quilting diagram

(Please see "Binding the Quilt," in "6 Quilting Makes the Quilt" if you need help.) As you come to the end of one length of quilt binding, you will need to piece in a new length of binding. Cover the ragged end with the folded-over end of the new length of binding. Blind stitch in place. Continue pinning. When the binding is pinned on all four sides, cut the binding end so as to leave 1" extra length. Turn this end under and stitch in place.

Step 3. Sew the pinned binding in place, using an appliqué stitch. Then turn your quilt over and do the same for the binding on the back. Add your name and the date, and your quilt will be finished!

About Doing Appliqué

Realistic and appliqué animals

Please read this section before beginning any of the appliqué projects (numbers 7 through 12). The directions offered here will make all of your projects easier.

Getting off to a Great Start

Before you do anything else, iron the fabric that you plan to use. If it is new fabric, iron out the fold that runs down the middle. If you are using fabric scraps, be sure to iron them flat. This is not just to make them look nice. The ironing is necessary to keep your drawing and cutting lines accurate.

Cutting the Templates

To begin your quilt, you will need to cut out one or more templates. A template is a pattern piece made from something stiff and sturdy—like cardboard or sandpaper. It is cut to the exact shape of the fabric pieces you will be cutting and sewing. You will use the template to trace the cutting and sewing lines for the fabric pieces themselves. Your templates must be made of a stiff material so they will hold up while you use them to trace the fabric shapes you need.

You will need a template for most of the fabric shapes for the projects offered here. Depending on the project, however, a few of the large background shapes may not require a template. You can cut these freehand according to the directions given for your project.

To cut out a template, follow the directions below. You will need these materials: tracing paper, pencil, and sandpaper or lightweight cardboard.

Step 1. If possible, use fine sandpaper for your templates instead of cardboard. The sandy side will cling to the fabric and your template will not slip as you trace around it. Also, you will be less likely to mix up the right and wrong sides of your template. (The following directions are for making and using sandpaper templates. If you cannot find any sandpaper, or if you can only find sandpaper with a slippery backing that is not good for drawing, just use cardboard. Be sure to make a mark on the right side of your cardboard so that you cannot get the right and wrong sides mixed up.)

Step 2. For each appliqué shape given in this book, there are two outlines. One is a thin outer line. The other is a thick inner line. The outer line is the *cutting* line. The inner line is the *folding* or *turning under* line. For each shape, trace both outlines onto the tracing paper exactly as they appear in the book. For now, ignore the short lines in between the two outlines.

Step 3. Turn your sandpaper sand side *down* (or your cardboard right side *down*). Hold the tracing paper so that the side on which you drew is facing down. Put the tracing paper on top of the sandpaper. Then retrace the lines you drew so that they

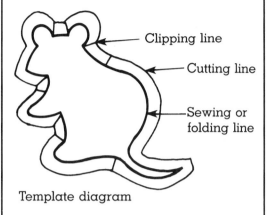

Template diagram

appear on the paper side of the sandpaper. Take the tracing paper away and darken the lines.

Step 4. Cut out each template carefully along the outer lines you have drawn.

Step 5. Label each template with the name of your project and the number of fabric shapes in each color needed to make your appliqué pattern.

Drawing and Cutting

Now you are ready to mark your fabric. You will be drawing the cutting lines on the fabric itself. Your template includes a seam allowance. This is the extra ¼" of fabric all around the outside of the inner line that "allows" you to turn under the edge of the appliqué shape.

Step 1. Place your fabric *right side down* on a flat work surface. A table or clean floor is fine.

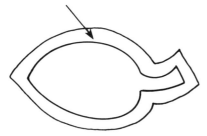

Appliqué seam allowance

Step 2. Put the template sand side *down* (or cardboard right side down) on the fabric. Place it so that the template is "with the grain" of the fabric. (The grain goes either from left to right or up and down. If you are not sure what this means, look closely at your fabric. You will see that it is made up of many tiny threads going from left to right and from top to bottom. "With the grain" means that the template is in line with these threads.)

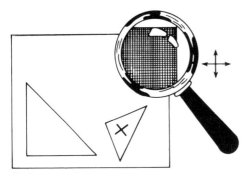

Fabric grain

Step 3. Draw around the outside of the template with a pencil. You have marked the cutting line of your first appliqué shape. Do the same for each appliqué shape you will need. Space the marked shapes as close together as possible so as not to waste fabric.

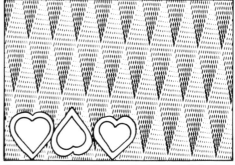

Space appliqué templates on fabric

Step 4. Re-cut your template, cutting on the inner line. Discard the extra ¼" all around your template. Your new, re-cut template will now be ¼" smaller all the way around.

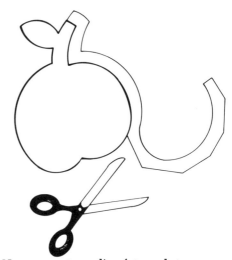

New, re-cut appliqué template

Step 5. For each appliqué shape, place the new, re-cut template in the center of the shape you have already drawn. It should be centered just right. Now draw a line around the outside of the new re-cut template. This will be your *folding* or *turning under* line. You will turn under and sew the edge of the appliqué shape all the way around so that the fold falls right on this line.

Step 6. Cut out each appliqué shape, cutting on the outer pencil line.

Step 7. Iron your shapes once they have been cut out.

Sewing the Shapes in Appliqué

Step 1. Turn to the page that shows the drawings of the templates with which you are working. Remember those short lines in between the two template outlines that you were told to ignore earlier? These are clipping lines. Using the drawing for your project as a guide, clip the fabric in the places where the clipping lines fall in the drawing. You need to do a little guesswork here. As long as your clips are similar to the clip lines as they appear in the drawing, they will be fine. Now you will be able to turn under the edges of the appliqué shapes.

Clipping

Step 2. Thread a regular "sharps" needle and knot one end. Do not double the thread. Sew with a single strand so your stitches will be almost impossible to see. Using a short basting stitch, fold under the edges of each appliqué shape and sew them lightly in place. Use thread that matches your fabric exactly. Take only tiny stitches on the right side of the fabric. Stitches on the wrong side of the fabric may be medium to large. You may want to pin under all the edges before you sew. Most people, however, prefer to sew as they turn the edge under with the thumb of the left hand and forefinger (for right-handed quilters).

Step 3. After all your shapes are sewn with the edges turned under, iron them carefully once again. If you do not iron them now, they may look crooked when you sew them in place on the background fabric.

Step 4. Using straight pins, pin your appliqué shapes in place on the background fabric. Use an appliqué stitch to sew each shape in place. Be sure to use thread that matches your appliqué fabric exactly. Use one strand of knotted thread in your needle. An appliqué stitch is done by bringing your needle up from back to front through the fold of the appliqué shape and pushing it back down through the background fabric. By losing the thread in the fold, you can make your stitches almost invisible.

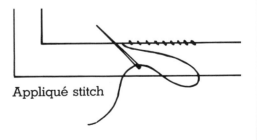

Appliqué stitch

Setting the Quilt

Depending on the project you are making, you may be working with more than one finished appliqué block. You will need to sew the blocks together. This is called *setting the quilt*.

Step 1. Begin by laying out all the blocks just as they are to appear in the finished project.

Step 2. Sew or join the blocks together in the order your project directions tell you to do. Generally, you will set them in pairs or groups of blocks, rather than in long rows. This makes it easier to match the seams.

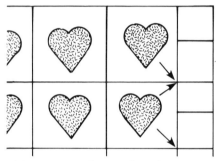

Matching seams for appliqué

Step 3. Match seams carefully as you sew. This means lining up the seams between all your blocks so that they meet evenly and form long lines of seams from one block to another. Say, for example, you want to sew two pairs of blocks to each other to make a square of four blocks. To do this, look at the seams from the front of the first pair. Now hold the first and second pair of blocks, right sides together, with the seams pressed against each other. Pin them in place from the back and turn the blocks around to the front to check your work. If the seams are matched properly, they will look like one long unbroken seam and may be sewn in place from the back with a running stitch (with the right sides still together).

Step 4. When the entire quilt is set, iron it on the wrong side of the fabric. Don't iron the seams open. Iron the light-colored seams toward dark-colored patches of fabric whenever possible. When you have finished ironing, you will be ready to do the actual quilting. Before you begin, please go back and read chapter "6 Quilting Makes the Quilt."

The Appliquéd Potholder

This easy appliqué project is similar in some ways to Project 1: The Pieced Potholder. Even if you have already completed the pieced potholder, you will find it helpful to make this project as a practice piece before going on to any of the other appliqué projects in this book.

Appliqué is very different from pieced work. The edges of each appliqué shape are turned under, and the shape is sewn onto a background fabric. The thread used must match the fabric of the appliqué shape exactly. Great care is taken not to let the stitches—other than quilting stitches—show.

Throughout the directions for the appliqué projects that follow, the word *background* is used to mean the fabric upon which an appliqué shape is sewn. *Backing* fabric continues to refer to the fabric that forms the back of an entire project.

There are two appliqué templates provided for this project. You can use either one. Or make a pair of potholders to give as a gift and use both templates. Stars and the moon were popular appliqué figures in old quilts. They reminded quilters of the beauty of the nighttime sky.

Don't forget to choose colors for your appliqué shapes that go well with the kitchen in which your potholders will appear!

Please read "13 About Doing Appliqué" before beginning this project.

⅓ yard of fabric A (white muslin)

⅓ yard of fabric B (calico)

Regular sewing thread to match each fabric (A and B) exactly

One 8″ square of background fabric. (This is the fabric on which the appliqué shape will be sewn. It is different from the project backing fabric. This square may be cut from the above piece of fabric A.)

One 10″ square of backing fabric. (This square may be cut from the above piece of fabric B.)

One 3-yard package of quilt binding

One metal ring

Quilting thread

Tracing paper

Fine sandpaper

Pencil

Scissors

Ruler

Needles (sharps and betweens)

Straight pins

Paper

One small embroidery hoop (4″ to 6″ diameter)

Tracing and Cutting

Step 1. There are two pattern templates for this project—the star and the moon. Choose one and, using a pencil, trace the template onto tracing paper. You will be tracing both a thin outer line and a thick inner line. The outer line will be the *cutting* line for your template. The inner line will be the *folding* or *turning under* line. (Remember, in appliqué, you must turn under the fabric shapes to hide the ragged edges.) For now, ignore the short lines between the cutting and folding lines. These are *clipping* lines and you will work with them later. They do not need to be marked on your fabric.

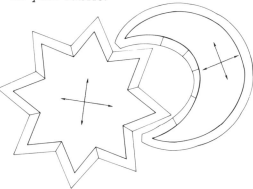

Step 2. Turn over the tracing paper and lay it on the smooth side of a piece of fine sandpaper. Retrace the pattern lines that show through on the wrong side of the tracing paper. The pattern will be transferred to the sandpaper below.

Step 3. Take away the tracing paper and darken your pattern lines so they are easy to see.

Step 4. With scissors, cut out the sandpaper template along the *outer* lines you have drawn.

Step 5. Place your piece of fabric B (calico) right side *down* on a flat work surface. Use your sandpaper template sand side *down* (or cardboard template right side down) to trace the *cutting* line for the appliqué shape you have chosen.

Step 6. Re-cut your template along the inner line. Your new, re-cut template should be ¼" smaller all the way around. Center it on the appliqué shape that you have traced. Trace around the outside of the new template to mark your *folding* line on the appliqué shape.

Step 7. The appliqué shape now has two lines around it. Cut it out on the outer *cutting* line, leaving the inner line as a folding and sewing guide.

Sewing the Design

Step 1. Iron your appliqué shape and your 8" square of background (not backing) fabric.

Step 2. Take another look at the template drawings for this project. Remember the short *clipping* lines between the cutting and folding lines? In order to be able to fold under the edges of your appliqué shape, you need to make short clips in the fabric. Look at the drawing for the appliqué shape you have chosen and clip your shape where the clip marks show in the drawing. You can guess at the places where the clips should fall. As long as you are close to what is shown in the drawing, your clips will be fine.

Step 3. To begin sewing, turn over the appliqué shape so the wrong side is facing you. Thread your sharps needle with a single, knotted strand of thread. Be sure the thread matches your appliqué shape fabric exactly. Use a short basting stitch to

sew the folded edges of the appliqué shape all the way around. Make the fold fall on the folding line you drew earlier. Most quilters prefer to fold the edge and hold it down, sewing it as they go. If you do not feel comfortable doing this, you may want to pin the folded edge of the appliqué shape first and then sew it all the way around.

Step 4. Pin the turned-under, sewn appliqué shape to the 8" square of background fabric.

Step 5. Once again, thread your needle with a single strand of knotted thread. The thread should match the appliqué shape exactly. Use an invisible or appliqué stitch to sew the shape in place. For an appliqué stitch, begin with your needle and knotted, single thread at the back of the piece. Bring the needle up to the top in the folded edge of the appliqué shape and put it back down very closely in the background fabric. Continue to bring the thread up, always letting it come through to the front by going through the fold in the appliqué shape. The stitches that show on the side of the appliqué should be tiny. The stitches that show on the back side of the background fabric, however, may be medium to large since they will not show. When you have finished sewing the appliqué shape to the background, your potholder appliqué block will be finished.

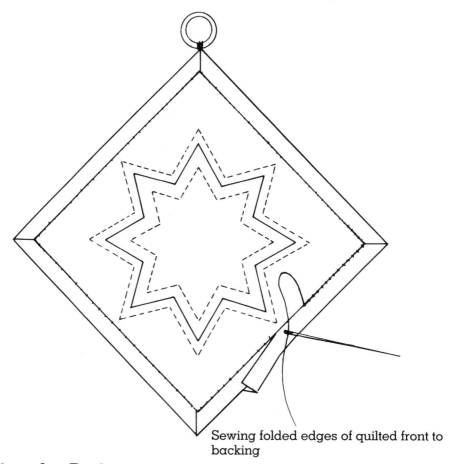

Sewing folded edges of quilted front to backing

Quilting the Project

Step 1. If you have not already done so, take a moment to read "6 Quilting Makes the Quilt."

Step 2. Iron the appliquéd block you have sewn.

Step 3. On a flat surface, place the 10″ square of backing fabric *right side down*. Place the batting over this. Next, place the ironed appliqué block *right side up* on these and center it. The same amount of extra batting and backing fabric should be sticking out from the appliqué block all the way around.

Step 4. Pin the potholder "sandwich" of backing fabric, batting, and appliqué block together in four or five places. Use a contrasting color of thread to baste the "sandwich" layers in place. Take large basting stitches—about 2″ each.

Step 5. Put the "sandwich" into the embroidery hoop. (This project is too small for a quilting hoop.) To do this, loosen the larger of the two embroidery hoop circles. Put the smaller of the two circles on your flat work surface, then place the potholder "sandwich" over the smaller circle and center it. Fit the larger circle down onto the smaller one, stretching the "sandwich" taut and flat between the two circles of the hoop.

Step 6. Thread a betweens quilting needle with a single strand of knotted quilting thread. (If you are new to quilting, you will want to use white thread, so that mistakes in stitching will be less likely to show.) Quilt evenly about ¼″ around the outside of the appliqué shape. Quilt all the way around the shape.

Step 7. Pin the quilting template for your project in the center of the matching appliqué shape. Quilt right next to the edge of the pinned template all the way around. When you are finished, knot your thread, lose the end of the thread in the batting, and clip. Unpin the template.

When you have finished the quilting, take the potholder out of the hoop and remove the basting stitches that hold the "sandwich" layers together.

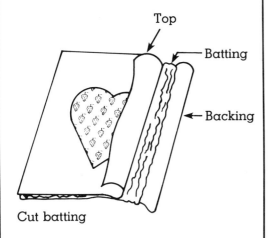

Cut batting

Fold

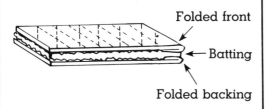

Folding front edge

Finishing Up

Step 1. Trim away the extra batting and backing fabric to make those layers even with the edges of your potholder top.

Step 2. You will use quilt binding to cover the ragged edge of the potholder. Pin one edge of the binding to the front edge of the potholder all the way around. At each corner, fold a little triangle of the binding under itself to make a diagonal seam. Pin in place. This is called mitering the corners. (Please see "Binding the Quilt" in chapter 6 if you need help.) At the end, cut the binding, making sure to leave one inch extra to hide the cut edges. Turn under, pin, and stitch.

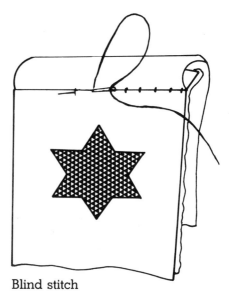

Blind stitch

Step 3. Use an appliqué stitch to sew the binding in place on the front of the potholder. Go back and sew the mitered corners.

Step 4. Turn the potholder over. Pin and sew the binding on the back just as you did on the front. Attach the metal ring on a corner for hanging.

Easy Eyeglass Case

Please read "13 About Doing Appliqué" before beginning this project.

Need a gift for someone who wears glasses or sunglasses? Here's the perfect project for you. Decorated with simple appliquéd hearts, it is easy to make.

The heart was a popular appliqué shape that appeared in many traditional quilts. In the old days, different kinds of hearts appeared in the quilts and folk art of different areas. For instance, Pennsylvania Dutch hearts were designed to be very wide. But the hearts that appeared in quilts from other parts of the country often were much more narrow.

For the background fabric on the outside of the eyeglass case, you may want to choose a solid color rather than white. An eyeglass case made from white muslin is likely to get dirty more quickly than one made from colored fabric. You may find that the best choice of fabrics are a calico and a solid of the same basic color, with a different solid color repeated from the calico for the inside or lining. For instance, the sample for this project uses blue-green calico with tiny pink flowers for the appliquéd hearts. Solid blue-green is used for the outside fabric, and solid pink (repeated in the calico flowers) forms the lining.

Tracing and Cutting

Step 1. There are two templates for this project—one for the main part of the case, and one for the appliquéd hearts. Trace the templates onto tracing paper. You will be tracing a thin outer line and a thick inner line.

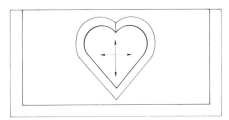

Materials

¼ yard of fabric A (blue-green calico)

¼ yard of fabric B (pink solid)

One 6″ × 10″ rectangle of fabric C, (a lightweight muslin. *Note:* This will be the backing for your quilting and will not show.)

One 12″ square of fabric D (blue-green calico)

One 6″ × 10″ rectangle of batting

Regular sewing thread to match fabrics A, B, and D exactly

Quilting thread

Tools

Tracing paper

Fine sandpaper

Pencil

Scissors

Ruler

Needles (sharps and betweens)

Straight pins

Paper

One medium-size embroidery hoop (6″ to 8″ diameter)

The outer line will be your *cutting* line. The inner line will be a *folding* line for the appliquéd hearts. For now, ignore the short clipping line at the top of the heart template.

Step 2. Turn the tracing paper over and lay it on the smooth side of a piece of fine sandpaper. Draw over the pattern lines that show through to the wrong side of the tracing paper. The pattern will be transferred to the sandpaper below.

Step 3. Take away the tracing paper and darken the pattern lines on the sandpaper.

Step 4. With scissors, cut out the sandpaper templates along the *outer* line you have drawn.

Step 5. Lay out the 12″ square of fabric D on a flat work surface, *right side down.* Use your sandpaper template to mark the *cutting* line for four hearts.

Step 6. Re-cut your template along the inner line. Your new, re-cut template should be ¼″ smaller all the way around. Center the template on each of the four hearts and trace around the new, smaller template to mark your *folding* line for each heart appliqué.

Step 7. Your appliqué hearts now have two lines around them. Cut them out on the outer *cutting* line, leaving the inner line as a folding guide.

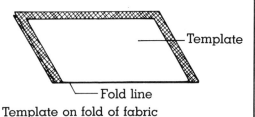

Template on fold of fabric

Step 8. Follow the same method for cutting out one rectangle from fabric A and one rectangle from fabric B. Fold your fabric in half. Be sure to place one long side of the rectangle template along this fold.

Sewing the Design

Step 1. Iron all of your cut and marked fabric shapes.

Step 2. Take a look at the template drawings for this project. Remember the short clipping line at the top of the heart? Looking at the drawing in the book, clip the heart appliqués accordingly.

Step 3. To begin sewing, take the first heart appliqué in hand so the wrong side is facing you. Thread your "sharps" needle with a single, knotted strand of thread that matches the heart fabric. Use a short basting stitch to sew under the folded edge of the appliqué shape all the way around. Make the fold fall on the folding line that you drew earlier. Turn under and baste the remaining hearts—and set them aside.

Step 4. Take the rectangle that is to be the outer part or background fabric of the eyeglass case. Fold it in half with the *right side out*. Position two of the hearts on each side as in the diagram. Pin the hearts in place.

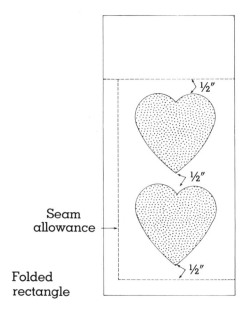

The hearts should be ½" apart. (Be sure to pin through only *one* layer of the folded background fabric.) Then turn the piece over and position the remaining two hearts in the same place on the other side. Open out the background fabric and lay it on the work surface.

Step 5. Once again, thread your needle with a single strand of knotted, matching thread and sew the hearts in place on the opened-out background fabric, using an appliqué stitch. (Remember, for an appliqué stitch, bring the thread up from the back so that it goes through the fold of the appliqué—and is almost impossible to see.)

Quilting the Project

Step 1. If you have not already done so, take a moment to read "6 Quilting Makes the Quilt."

Step 2. Iron the appliquéd heart rectangle that you have sewn.

Step 3. On your work surface, lay out the backing fabric rectangle (the piece that will not show) *right side down*. On top of this, center the rectangle of batting. Place the heart rectangle *right side up* on these and center it in place. There should be about the same amount of extra batting and backing fabric sticking out beyond the heart rectangle all the way around.

Step 4. Pin the eyeglass case "sandwich" of backing fabric, batting, and appliquéd rectangle in five or six places. Use a contrasting color of thread to baste the layers together. Use long basting stitches—about 1" or 2" each.

Step 5. Put the "sandwich" into the embroidery hoop so that one of the four hearts is in the center of the hoop.

Quilting diagram

Step 6. Using a betweens quilting needle and heavy quilting thread, take tiny stitches around the inside of the heart. The line of quilting should be about ¼" inside the edge of the heart and will make a little heart of quilting stitches. Next, quilt all the way around the outside of the heart appliqué—¼" from the edge. This will make a second heart of quilting stitches. Run an additional line of quilting stitches ¼" outside the

second heart to make a third heart of quilting stitches. Do the same for each of the remaining heart appliqués. You will have to replace your "sandwich" in the hoop to reach all of the hearts. When you are done quilting, take the "sandwich" out of the hoop and remove the basting stitches.

Finishing Up

Step 1. Trim away the extra batting and backing fabric to make them even with the edges of the heart rectangle.

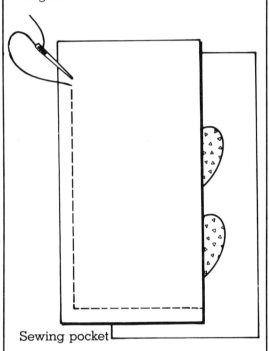

Sewing pocket

Step 2. Fold the heart rectangle in half so that the hearts are facing in. Sew a seam, joining the front and back of the case down the long side (opposite the folded side) and along the bottom of the folded rectangle. This will make a kind of *pocket*. Now your project is beginning to look like an eyeglass case. Set this pocket aside.

Step 3. Fold the lining in half with the right side in. Run a seam, joining the front and back of the lining, down the long side (opposite the folded side) and along the bottom of the folded rectangle—just as you did before—to make another pocket. When this lining pocket is sewn, turn it right side out.

Step 4. Measure 2″ down from the top ragged edge of the lining pocket. In pencil, lightly mark a line all along the top part of the pocket, back and front, 2″ down from the top edge. This line will be your folding line. Fold the top edge in and under along this line. (The ragged edge should be on the inside of the lining pocket.) Pin the folded edge in place from the outside of the lining.

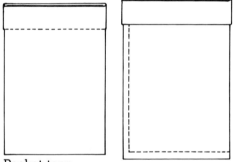

Pocket tops

Step 5. Measure 1½″ down from the ragged edge of the heart pocket (the first pocket you sewed). Lightly, in pencil, mark this line all along the top part of the heart pocket 1½″ from the top edge. Fold the top edge out and baste it in place along the ragged edge. (This time, the ragged edge will be on the outside of the pocket.) The basting stitches should not go above the ½″ sewing line you marked earlier. Also, as you baste, do not run the thread all the way through the three layers of this pocket. Let the thread run no farther than the batting layer.

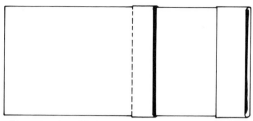

Positioning lining

Step 6. Let's stop for a moment and check your work. At this point, the lining pocket should be turned right side out, with the top folded edge pinned. The pins should be showing so that they can be pulled out easily. The heart pocket should be turned right side in, with the top edge turned out and basted in place. Fit the lining pocket over the heart pocket. This means that the heart pocket will be inside the lining pocket.

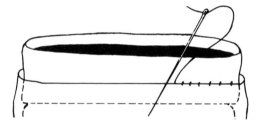

Step 7. Adjust the top of the pinned lining pocket so it covers the basting stitches along the top of the heart pocket. One at a time, remove each pin from the lining pocket and re-pin the top edge of the lining pocket to hide the basting stitches of the heart pocket.

Step 8. Using an appliqué stitch and thread that matches the lining fabric exactly, sew the *turned under* edge of the lining pocket to the *turned out* edge of the heart pocket. When this is done, turn the finished eyeglass case right side out. You may want to take one or two stitches at each bottom corner of the case to hold the lining in place. This will keep the lining from pulling out when the glasses are removed from the case.

Project 9—easy

Schoolhouse Mini Quilt

Please read chapter "13 About Doing Appliqué" before beginning this project.

The schoolhouse was an important building in early America. Today, a basic education is something we often take for granted. But our ancestors did not feel that way. One reason many people first came to this country was to have the right to educate their children as they thought best. Nearly every frontier town had its own little red schoolhouse.

The Schoolhouse pattern became very popular for quilts. In fact, it became so popular that there is both a pieced and an appliqué pattern called The Schoolhouse. The appliqué Schoolhouse is a little easier and has fewer pieces to work with than the pieced version. That is why it is included here.

Miniature quilts, like the one in this project, offer a fun, quick way to enjoy quilting. A mini quilt may be displayed on a wall like a wall hanging. Or you might want to make one for a younger sister's favorite doll—or even for an adult who collects dolls.

Materials

½ yard of fabric A (white muslin)

¼ yard of fabric B (blue calico)

¼ yard of fabric C (pink calico)

Regular sewing thread to match the appliqué fabrics (B and C) exactly

Enough fabric scraps to make thirty-six 2½″ squares (assorted colors)

One package of ¾″ blue calico bias tape

One 24″ square of batting

One 24″ square of backing fabric

Quilting thread

Tools

Tracing paper

Fine sandpaper

Pencil

Scissors

Ruler

Needles (sharps and betweens)

Straight pins

Paper

One small quilting hoop (14″ diameter)

Tracing and Cutting

Step 1. There are five templates for this project—two for the schoolhouse, plus a large square, a small square, and a heart. Trace them all onto tracing paper. For each, you will be tracing a thin outer line and a thick inner line. The outer line will be your *cutting* line. The inner line will be a *folding* line for the appliqué shapes and a *sewing* line for the squares. For now, ignore the short clipping lines in the drawings between the cutting and folding or sewing lines.

Step 2. Turn the tracing paper over and lay it on the smooth side of a piece of fine sandpaper. Draw over the pattern lines that show through the wrong side of the tracing paper. The pattern will be transferred to the sandpaper below.

Step 3. Take away the tracing paper and darken the pattern lines on the sandpaper.

Step 4. With scissors, cut out the sandpaper templates along the *outer* lines you have drawn.

Step 5. For all the templates except the small square, lay out the fabrics on a flat work surface, *right side down.* Use your sandpaper template sand side down (or cardboard template right side down) to trace the cutting lines for the following:

> 16 large squares from fabric A
> 12 schoolhouse buildings from fabric B
> 12 schoolhouse roofs from fabric B
> 4 hearts from fabric C

Step 6. After all of the pieces are marked on the fabrics, re-cut each template along the inner line. Your new, re-cut templates will be ¼" smaller all the way around. Center each template on the correct fabric shape that you traced. Then trace around the new, smaller template to mark your *folding* (or sewing) line on the appliqué shape.

Step 7. Your appliqué shapes now have two lines around them. Cut them out on the outer *cutting* lines, leaving the inner lines as a folding and sewing guide.

Step 8. Iron and lay out your scraps for the pieced border of the mini quilt—all *right side down*. Use the small square template to mark each of the small scrap squares. Re-cut the template and mark the sewing lines on the scrap squares. Then cut them out as you did the above shapes.

Sewing the Design

Step 1. Iron all the cut-out fabric shapes.

Step 2. Take a look at the template drawings for this project. Remember the short clipping lines between the cutting and folding lines? Looking at the drawings in the book, clip your heart and schoolhouse appliqués accordingly.

Step 3. To begin sewing the schoolhouses, take the first schoolhouse appliqué shape in hand so the wrong side is facing you. Thread your "sharps" needle with a single, knotted strand of thread that matches the schoolhouse fabric. Use a short basting stitch to sew under the folded edge of the appliqué shape all the way around. Make the fold fall on the folding line that you drew earlier. Turn under and baste the twelve schoolhouses and their roofs. Set them aside.

Step 4. Turn under and baste each of the heart appliqué shapes, using matching thread. Set these aside as well.

Step 5. Pin each schoolhouse and its roof in the center of a large square. Position the roof so there is a ⅛" space between the schoolhouse building and its roof. Pin each of the four hearts to a large square, just as you did for the schoolhouse.

Step 6. Once again, thread your needle with a single strand of knotted thread to match first the schoolhouse and then the heart appliqué. Sew the appliqué shapes to the large background squares or blocks, using an appliqué stitch. As each miniature appliqué block is finished, set it aside.

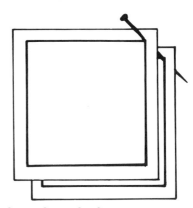

Pin-through method

Step 7. The miniature appliquéd quilt has a pieced border. Sew ten of the small fabric squares into a row to begin the border. Next, make another row of ten squares and then piece two rows of eight squares. Remember to use your pin to help line up the sewing lines. To do this, line up the first two squares with right sides together. Run your pin through the sewing line of the square facing you.

Be sure it comes out through the sewing line of the square facing away from you. If the pin is off the sewing line on the square facing away from you, adjust the position of the two squares. Do this at two or three points along the sewing line. When you are sure the sewing lines match up on either side, pin the squares together and sew them along one edge, using a running stitch.

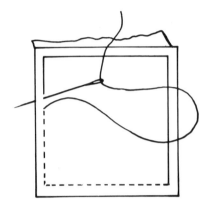

Setting the Quilt

Step 1. Iron the miniature appliqué blocks and the four pieced rows of border squares.

Step 2. On a flat surface, lay out the ironed pieces as they will appear in the finished mini quilt.

Step 3. You will be sewing together three schoolhouse blocks and a heart block into a square made up of four blocks. You will need to do this four times. Begin by sewing two blocks into a pair. Remember to use your pin to help line up the sewing lines. Go on and sew another pair of blocks. Then, matching the seams between the two pairs of blocks, with right sides together, line up and sew the pairs to make a square of four blocks.

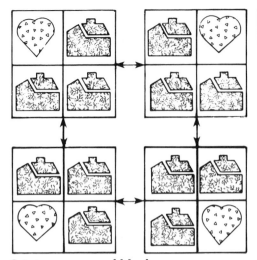

Joining groups of blocks

Step 4. Do the same for the remaining blocks—joining them into a total of four squares of four blocks each. Remember to use your pin to help you line up the sewing lines and be sure to match the seams between the blocks as you go.

Step 5. Sew the four squares of blocks into a single square of sixteen blocks, using the methods described above. Remember to use your pin to line up the sewing lines of the blocks and match seams carefully as you go.

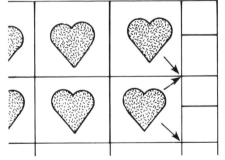

Matching seams

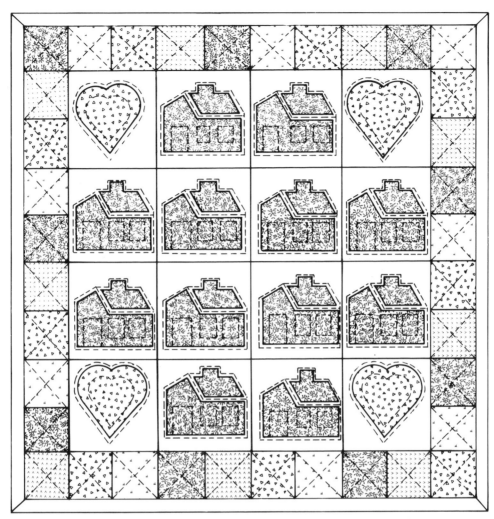

Mini quilt sewing and quilting diagram

Step 6. Now you are ready to sew the border of squares to the joined schoolhouse blocks. Find the middle seam of one of the ten-square border rows. With right sides together, match this seam to the middle seam of one side of the schoolhouse blocks section. Use your pin to help you line up the sewing lines along the row. Pin the first row of squares to the schoolhouse section and use a running stitch to sew in place.

Step 7. On the opposite side of the schoolhouse section of the quilt, match the middle seams, then pin and sew the other ten-square border row. On either remaining side, sew the two eight-square rows, starting in the middle. Sew the loose squares at each corner with right sides together, using a running stitch.

Quilting the Project

Step 1. If you have not already done so, take a moment to read "6 Quilting Makes the Quilt."

Step 2. Iron the mini quilt top you have sewn.

Step 3. On a flat surface, place the 24" backing fabric square *right side down*. Put the square of batting on top of this. Place the ironed mini quilt top, centered and right side up, on these. There should be the same amount of extra batting and backing fabric sticking out beyond the mini quilt top all the way around.

Step 4. Pin the mini quilt "sandwich" of schoolhouse pattern, batting, and backing in eight or nine places. Use a contrasting color of thread to baste the layers together. Take long basting stitches—about 2" each.

Step 5. Put the mini quilt "sandwich" into the quilting hoop. You will want to quilt the center first.

Step 6. Using a "betweens" quilting needle and heavy quilting thread, take tiny stitches around the outside of each schoolhouse and each heart. You may also want to add a quilted door and window to your schoolhouse—and an inner quilted heart within the fabric heart. The quilting around the outside of each appliqué shape should be about 1/8" from the edge of the appliqué. Run a line of quilting between each schoolhouse building and its roof too, if you like. You may have to replace your quilt "sandwich" in the hoop to reach all of the blocks.

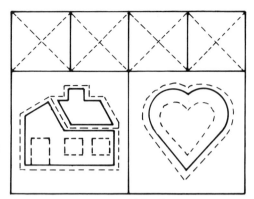

Quilting diagram of blocks

Step 7. When the blocks are done, it is time to quilt the border squares. You may find it is easier to do this without the quilting hoop. Put short strips of masking tape on the squares and quilt one diagonal at a time to form a quilted X across each border square. When you have quilted all of the squares, remove the "sandwich" from the hoop (if you are still using it) and take out the basting stitches.

Finishing Up

Step 1. Trim away the extra batting and backing fabric to make them even with the edges of your mini quilt top.

Step 2. You will use the bias tape to cover the ragged edge of your mini quilt. Pin one edge of the bias tape to the front edge of your quilt all the way around. As you come to each corner, fold the tape so it makes a little triangle of fabric under itself. This will make a diagonal seam show at the corner—like on a picture frame. This is called *mitering* the corner.

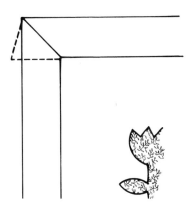

(Please review "Binding the Quilt" from "6 Quilting Makes the Quilt" if you need help.) Pin each mitered corner as you go. When you have pinned the bias tape on all four sides, leave about 3" of extra tape at the end and cut off the rest.

Step 3. Using an appliqué stitch, sew the bias tape to the top of the quilt edge all the way around. Go back and sew each mitered corner separately.

Step 4. Pin the other edge of the bias tape to the back of the mini quilt and sew in place. To finish, cut the extra tape so there is only about ½" extra. Turn under ¼" of this and stitch the end of the bias tape down to complete your mini quilt. Remember to add your name and the date on the back.

Design-Your-Own Wall Quilt

In this project, you will be using fabric *silhouettes* to create a wall quilt that is just like a quilted picture. Have you ever seen an old-fashioned silhouette? A silhouette is a one-color, filled-in outline of a person, animal, or object. In the old days, before photography, rich people often hired an artist to paint their portraits. People who were not wealthy hired a silhouette maker. The traveling silhouette artist would cut a silhouette of his subject's profile and shoulders from a piece of black paper and mount it on a white background.

In this project, you will be working with a different kind of silhouette. Your silhouettes will be made of fabric, and they will be silhouettes of animals, trees, and farmhouses. Many of the old-time quilters used silhouetted figures like these in their own "picture-style" quilts.

The most important ingredient in making a successful silhouette is *contrast*. Two things contrast when one stands out sharply against the other. You will want your fabric silhouettes to stand out sharply against the background in your wall quilt. To make this happen, you will use dark calico for the background and light, solid-colored fabrics for the silhouettes.

This project is called "design your own" because you will be given a range of silhouettes from which to choose to make your wall quilt. You can use the ones from the sample for this project or try different ones from the additional templates included.

Please read chapter "13 About Doing Appliqué" before beginning this project.

Old-fashioned silhouette

Also, the project calls for using green background strips of calico to create the effect of green hills and fields in summer. Instead, you might want to use brown or gold calicoes to create an autumn landscape. Although the directions include the colors from the sample for this project, feel free to use your own colors and to experiment a little!

Remember, you often can buy "quilter's quarters" or pre-cut quarter yards of calico at fabric stores. Before you buy, ask the fabric store attendant about the length of the quarters and be sure they are at least 22" long—the length you need for this project.

Tracing and Cutting

Step 1. Begin by preparing the silhouette figures for your project. There are a number of templates for this project. Decide which silhouettes you want to use. Then trace the chosen ones onto tracing paper. For each, you will be tracing a thin outer line and a thick inner line. The outer line will be your *cutting* line. The inner line will be your *folding* line. For now, ignore the short, clipping lines in the drawings between the two outlines.

Materials

One 22" × 10" strip of solid light blue fabric

One 22" × 9" strip of dark green calico

Six different 22" × 3" green calico strips ranging from medium to dark

Solid-color fabric scraps for the silhouette appliqué figures you choose. To follow the sample exactly, you will need:

> One 12" square of light red
> One 12" square of white
> One 6" square of light brown
> One 6" square of dark red

Regular sewing thread to match each silhouette appliqué fabric

One 22" square of lightweight muslin

One 24" square of batting

One 24" square of backing fabric

One 4-yard package of light blue quilt binding

Quilting thread

Tools

Tracing paper
Fine sandpaper
Pencil
Scissors
Ruler
Dressmaker's chalk
Needles (sharps and
　　betweens)
Straight pins
Paper
One small quilting hoop (14″
　　diameter)

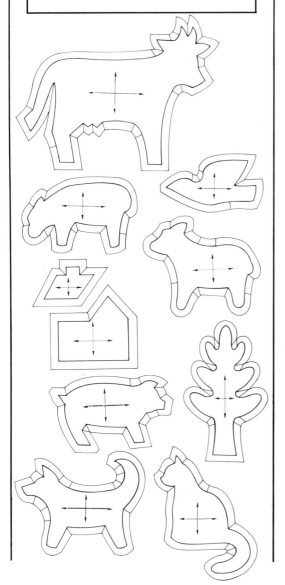

Step 2. Turn over the tracing paper and lay it on the smooth side of a piece of fine sandpaper. Draw over the pattern lines that show through the wrong side of the tracing paper. The pattern will be transferred to the sandpaper below.

Step 3. Take away the tracing paper and darken the pattern lines on the sandpaper.

Step 4. With scissors, cut out the sandpaper templates along the *outer* lines you have drawn.

Step 5. For all the templates, lay out the fabrics you will be working with on a flat work surface, *right side down.* Use your sandpaper template *sand side down* (or cardboard template right side down) to trace your cutting lines. To follow the sample project exactly, trace the cutting lines for the following:

> One light red cow
> Two white sheep
> One light brown sheep
> One dark red farmhouse

Step 6. After marking the shape needed, re-cut your template along the inner line. Your new, re-cut template should be ¼″ smaller all the way around. Center each template on the correct fabric shape that you already traced. Then trace around the new, smaller template to mark the *folding* line on the appliqué shape.

Step 7. Your appliqué shapes now have two lines around them. Cut them out on the outer *cutting* line, leaving the inner lines as a folding and sewing guide.

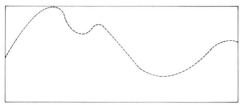

Cutting

Step 8. Next, you will work with the dark green calico that forms the background hills for your landscape. Use a piece of dressmaker's chalk (available at most fabric stores) to mark a cutting line on the 22" × 9" dark green strip of calico. Begin by putting the strip on your work surface *right side down*. Draw the cutting line freehand, using the diagram included with the templates for this project as a visual guide. Your cutting line does not need to match the diagram exactly. If you do not like the first cutting line that you draw, brush the chalk off the fabric and draw another one. When you are satisfied with your cutting line, use your scissors to cut out the piece, following the line you have drawn.

Step 9. Next, you will work with the six green calicoes that form the fields of the landscape. Trim each of the 22" × 3" green calicoes to make their widths all slightly different. (See the sample for this project. You will see that each strip is a little different from the ones around it. This gives the feeling of green hills in the distance. You can give your landscape the same feeling by drawing a trim line freehand on the wrong side of each strip and cutting out the pieces so they all have slightly different widths.)

Sewing the Design

Step 1. Iron all the silhouette fabric figures and all the strips for this project.

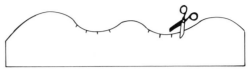

Clipping

Step 2. Take a look at the template drawings for this project. Remember the short clipping lines between the cutting and folding lines? Looking at the drawings in the book, clip your fabric silhouettes accordingly. Then make similar clips in the curved parts of the hill strip and field strips of calico. You will only need to clip the parts that curve inward.

Step 3. To begin sewing the silhouettes, thread your needle with a single, knotted strand of thread to match the first silhouette you will work with. Hold the silhouette so that the wrong side is facing you, fold on the folding line, and take short basting stitches all around the edge. Do the same for each of the silhouette figures; set them aside.

Step 4. Lay out the landscape background strips of fabric in the following order from top to bottom: blue sky strip, dark green, faraway hills strip, and six green field strips from lightest to darkest. Using a single knotted strand of matching thread, turn under and baste *the top edge only* of each green strip. (Do not sew the blue sky strip at all. Just leave it in place.) Lay each basted strip back down in place in the correct order as it is finished. When all the strips are basted, iron them carefully.

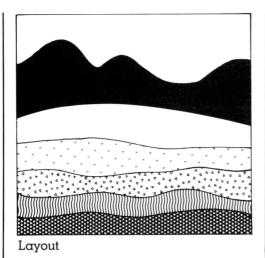

Layout

Step 5. On your work surface, lay out the 22" square of lightweight muslin. You will be covering the muslin with the landscape background strips, working from top to bottom. Arrange the strips on the muslin in the order you worked with above, starting with the sky at the top and finishing with the darkest green field strip at the bottom. When you have the strips arranged the way you like them, pin them in place. Be sure each basted edge of one strip hides the ragged edge of the strip above it.

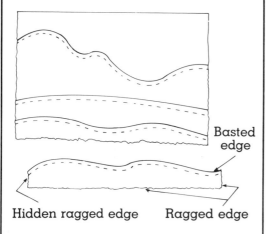

Basted edge

Hidden ragged edge   Ragged edge

Step 6. Use a single knotted strand of matching thread and an appliqué stitch to sew the pinned landscape strips in place. (Remember, for an appliqué stitch, you bring the needle up from the back through the fold of the turned-under fabric edge.)

Step 7. When the entire background landscape has been sewn in place on the muslin, you are ready to arrange your silhouette figures the way you want them to appear. Pin them in place on the background and sew. Use a single, knotted strand of matching thread and an appliqué stitch.

Quilting the Project

Step 1. If you have not already done so, take a moment to read "6 Quilting Makes the Quilt."

Step 2. Iron the wall quilt top you have sewn.

Step 3. On a flat surface, place the 24" backing fabric square *right side down*. Put the square of batting on top of this. Place the ironed wall quilt top, centered and *right side up*, on these. There should be about the same amount of extra batting and backing fabric sticking out beyond the wall quilt top all the way around.

Step 4. Pin the wall quilt "sandwich" of backing, batting, and landscape picture in eight or nine places. Use a contrasting color of thread to baste the layers together. Take long basting stitches—about 2" each.

Step 5. Put the wall quilt "sandwich" into the quilting hoop. You will want to quilt the calico strips first and go on to quilt the silhouette figures last.

Step 6. Using a betweens quilting needle and heavy quilting thread, take tiny stitches just inside the edge of each strip. Quilt each strip in order, beginning with the top and ending with the bottom. Reposition your wall quilt "sandwich" in the hoop as needed.

Step 7. When all the strips are quilted, quilt around the outside of each silhouette figure. Your line of quilting here should be about ¼" from the outside edge of the silhouette. Reposition your "sandwich" in the hoop as needed. When you have finished quilting, take the "sandwich" out of the hoop and remove the basting stitches.

Finishing Up

Step 1. Trim away the extra batting and backing fabric to make them even with the edges of your wall quilt top.

Step 2. You will use the quilt binding to cover the ragged edge of your wall quilt. Pin one edge of the quilt binding to the front of your quilt all the way around. As you come to each corner, fold the binding so it makes a little triangle of fabric under itself. This will make a diagonal seam show at the corner—like on a picture frame. (This is called *mitering* the corner. Please review "Binding the Quilt" from "6 Quilting Makes the Quilt" if you need help.) Pin each mitered corner as you go. When you have pinned the binding on all four sides, leave about 3" of extra binding at the end and cut off the rest.

Step 3. Using an appliqué stitch, sew the binding to the top of the quilt edge all the way around. Go back and sew each mitered corner separately.

Step 4. Pin the other edge of the binding to the back of the wall quilt and sew in place. To finish, cut the excess binding so there is only about 1" extra. Turn ½" of this under and stitch down the end of the binding to complete your wall quilt. Be sure to add your name and the date to the back.

Step 5. If you like, you can make fabric loops for hanging your wall quilt from the leftover quilt binding. Cut four 4" lengths of binding. Pin them to the top of the wall quilt so there is the same amount of space between each. Pin in place so that the ragged ends of the binding are folded and hidden underneath the binding itself. Then sew in place. A wooden dowel (available at most hardware stores) can be inserted through the loops for hanging your finished wall quilt.

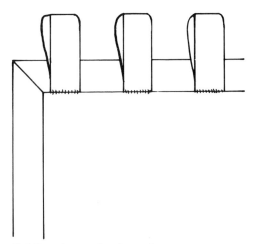

Adding loops for hanging

Cat in the Window Wall Quilt

Please read chapter "13 About Doing Appliqué" before beginning this project.

This project is similar in some ways to the Design-Your-Own Wall Quilt that came before. In this project, you will use calico to form hills and fields in the background of the design. There is also a fabric silhouette in the shape of a cat. This wall quilt is a little more challenging to make than the one before it because it has a border—and extra quilt binding is used to outline the windowpane.

In choosing colors for your wall quilt, be sure to remember *contrast*. You will want to be sure your cat silhouette stands out well from the rest of the design. One way to do this is to use gray-green calicoes for the landscape hills and bright orange calico for the cat. The directions for this project include the colors used in the sample, but feel free to use your own colors.

If you decide to use "quilter's quarters" or pre-cut quarter yard pieces of calico from your fabric store, be sure they are at least 18″ long—the length you need for this project.

Tracing and Cutting

Step 1. There are six templates for this project—the cat, the border triangle, hilltop, and three templates to form the road. Trace all of the templates onto tracing paper. For each, you will be tracing a thin outer line and a thick inner line. The outer line will be your *cutting* line. The inner line will be your *folding* line. For now, ignore the short clipping lines in the drawings between the two outlines.

Tools

Tracing paper
Fine sandpaper
Pencil
Scissors
Ruler
Dressmaker's chalk
Needles (sharps and
	betweens)
Straight pins
Paper
One small quilting hoop (14″
	in diameter)

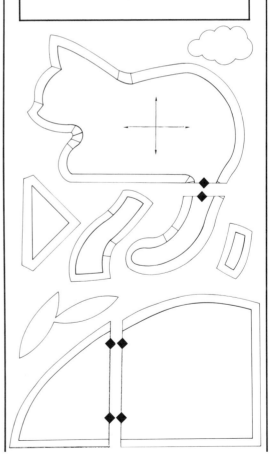

Materials

One 18″ × 12″ strip of solid
	light blue fabric
One 12″ × 6″ piece of dark
	green calico
One 18″ × 6″ strip of medium
	green calico
One 18″ × 6″ strip of medium
	solid green fabric
One 18″ × 12″ strip of light
	green calico
One 18″ × 12″ strip of solid
	brown
One 12″ square of orange
	calico
One 12″ square of dark red
	or maroon calico
½ yard of regular-weight
	white muslin
One 18″ × 21″ piece of
	lightweight muslin (this
	piece will not show)
One 36″ square of batting
One 36″ square of backing
	fabric
Three 3-yard packages of
	dark red or maroon quilt
	binding
Regular sewing thread to
	match the appliqué fabrics
	and quilt binding exactly
Quilting thread

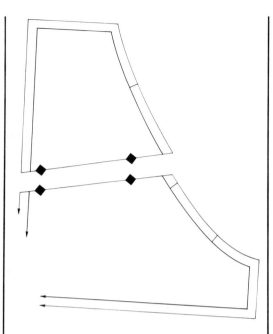

Step 2. Turn over the tracing paper and lay it on the smooth side of a piece of fine sandpaper. Draw over the pattern lines that show through the wrong side of the tracing paper. The pattern will be transferred to the sandpaper below.

Step 3. Take away the tracing paper and darken the pattern lines on the sandpaper.

Step 4. With scissors, cut out the sandpaper templates along the *outer* lines you have drawn.

Step 5. For all the templates, lay out the fabrics on a flat work surface, *right side down*. Be sure to use your sandpaper template *sand side down* (or cardboard template right side down) to mark your cutting lines.

Step 6. After you have marked the cutting lines on the fabric, re-cut your template along the inner line. Your new, re-cut template should be ¼" smaller all the way around. Center each template on the correct fabric shape that you already traced. Then trace around the new,

smaller template to mark your *folding* line on the appliqué shapes. *Note:* This line will be a *sewing* line for the pieced triangles.

Step 7. Your fabric shapes now have two lines around them. Cut them out on the outer *cutting* line, leaving the inner line as a folding and sewing guide.

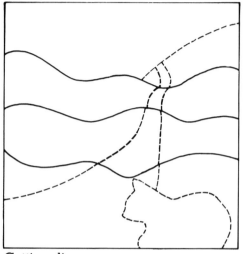

Cutting diagram

Step 8. Next, you will work with the fabrics that form the sky and hills for your landscape. Place the blue sky strip on your work surface. Next, arrange the three long green fabric strips from lightest at the top (below the sky) to darkest at the bottom. Use a piece of dressmaker's chalk to mark a cutting line on each green strip. Mark the cutting line freehand, using the fabric cutting diagram for this project as a visual guide. Your cutting line does not need to match the diagram exactly. When you are satisfied with the cutting lines you have marked, use your scissors to cut out the pieces.

Step 9. Cut four strips of regular white muslin 19" × 4" each. Use a pencil and ruler to mark a ½" seam allowance on all four sides of each strip.

Sewing the Design

Step 1. Iron all the cut fabric shapes for this project.

Step 2. Take a look at the template drawings for this project. Remember the short clipping lines between the cutting and folding lines? Look at the drawings in the book and clip your appliqué shapes accordingly. Then make similar clips in the curved parts of the green calico hill strips. You will only need to clip the parts that curve inward.

Step 3. To begin sewing the appliqué shapes, thread your needle with a single, knotted strand of thread to match the cat silhouette. Hold the cat shape so that the wrong side is facing you. Fold on the folding line and take small basting stitches all the way around the edge. Be sure to take tiny stitches on the right side of the fabric—the side that will show. When you are done, set the cat appliqué aside.

Step 4. Lay out the landscape background fabric shapes in the following order from top to bottom: blue sky strip, dark green hilltop, medium green calico strip, medium green solid strip, and light green calico strip. Using a single knotted strand of matching thread, turn under and baste *the top edge only* of each strip or shape. Lay down the pieces in the correct order as they are finished. When all the pieces are basted, iron them carefully.

Step 5. On your work surface, lay out the 18″ × 21″ piece of lightweight muslin. You will be covering the muslin with the landscape background pieces, working from top to bottom. Arrange the strips on the muslin in the order you worked with

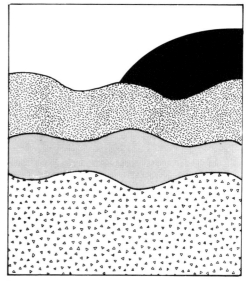

Layout diagram

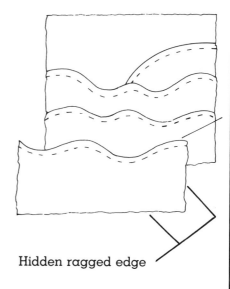

Hidden ragged edge

above, starting with the sky at the top and finishing with the light green calico strip at the bottom. When you have the strips arranged the way you like them, pin them in place. Be sure that the basted edge of each strip hides the ragged edge of the strip above it.

129

Step 6. Use a single, knotted strand of matching thread and an appliqué stitch to sew the pinned landscape strips in place. (Remember, for an appliqué stitch, you bring the needle up from the back through the fold of the turned-under fabric edge.)

Step 7. When the entire background landscape has been sewn in place on the lightweight muslin, you are ready to complete the remaining parts of the picture. Turn under and baste the three brown road fabric shapes all the way around. Iron the basted pieces carefully. Pin the basted road shapes in place on the landscape, but do not sew them down.

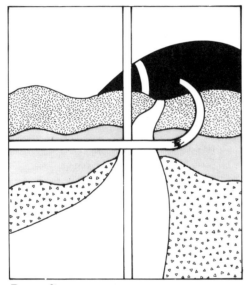

Pane diagram

Step 8. You are now going to pin strips of the quilt binding to make the "window panes" for your quilt picture. Run a strip of quilt binding down the center of the landscape scene from top to bottom. Measure to be sure you have the exact center.

Then pin the strip of binding in place. Do the same, using a second strip of binding running from left to right. Adjust your "road" fabric strips so that the ragged edges of the road are covered by the quilt binding.

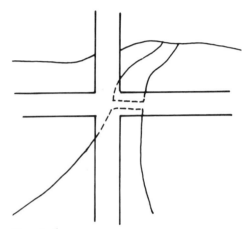

Road diagram

Step 9. Sew the road and the "windowpane" quilt binding in place, using matching thread and an appliqué stitch.

Step 10. Pin and sew a border of quilt binding all the way around the landscape scene. You will need to miter each of the corners as you come to them. To do this, fold the binding so it makes a little triangle of fabric under itself at each corner. This will make a diagonal seam show at the corner—like on a picture frame. (If you need help, please see about mitering the corner under "Binding the Quilt" from chapter "6 Quilting Makes the Quilt.")

Step 11. Pin the basted and ironed cat silhouette on the landscape scene so that the bottom of the cat rests on the bottom border of quilt binding—as if it were sitting on the sill of your "window." Then, use a single strand of knotted, matching thread and an appliqué stitch to sew the cat in place. Do not stitch the cat's tail. That will come later. For now, just let the tail hang loosely or pin it up out of the way.

Step 12. Use the pieced-work techniques you learned earlier to sew the border triangles into four squares of four triangles each. (You may want to review "5 About Doing Pieced Work.")

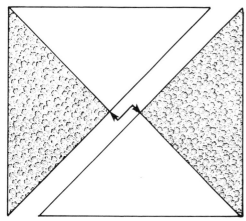

Pieced corners

Step 13. Join one long white muslin strip to each side of the landscape scene. When you have sewn the bottom muslin strip in place, pin and stitch the cat's tail so it comes down over the muslin. Join a square of triangles at each corner formed by the muslin strips.

Quilting the Project

Step 1. If you have not already done so, take a moment to read "6 Quilting Makes the Quilt."

Step 2. Iron the wall quilt top you have sewn.

Step 3. On a flat surface, place the 36" backing fabric square *right side down*. Put the square of batting on top of this. Place the ironed wall quilt top, centered and *right side up*, on these. Trim the extra batting and backing so that there is about 3" extra sticking out beyond the quilt top on all sides.

Step 4. Pin the wall quilt "sandwich" of quilt top, batting, and backing fabric in ten or twelve places. Use a contrasting color of thread to baste the layers together. Take long basting stitches—about 2" each. Remove the pins.

Step 5. Put the wall quilt "sandwich" into the quilting hoop. You will want to quilt the center area of the design first and go on to the muslin border last.

Step 6. Using a betweens quilting needle and heavy quilting thread, take tiny stitches just inside the edge of each "hill" strip. Quilt each strip in order, beginning with the top and ending with the bottom. Reposition your wall quilt "sandwich" in the hoop as needed.

Step 7. When all the "hill" strips are quilted, quilt ¼" around the *outside* of the cat. This means you will have to run a line of quilting along part of the red binding border in order to quilt around the cat's tail—but this is okay. Finally, quilt a center line down the middle of the brown "road."

Step 8. Trace the cloud and the double leaf *quilting* templates for this project onto tracing paper and transfer them to plain paper. Cut them out. Pin the cloud template in place on the "sky." Then quilt around it, using it as a guide. You may want to replace it several times on the sky to make three or more quilted "clouds" as in the project sample.

Wall hanging sewing and quilting diagram

Step 9. You may find that it is easier to do the final quilting without the hoop. If so, just hold the wall quilt "sandwich" in one hand and take your stitches with the other. Pin the double leaf template at the bottom of one strip of the white muslin border. Quilt all the way around it, then re-pin it so the tip barely touches the leaf design you have just quilted. Do this all along the first strip of muslin,

adjusting the quilting template so that you do not end up with half a leaf. Follow the same method for the other three muslin strips that form the border.

Step 10. Finally, quilt each corner square of triangles. You will want to quilt ¼" *inside* each triangle. When all the quilting is done, remove the basting stitches.

Finishing Up

Step 1. Trim away the extra batting and backing fabric to make them even with the edges of your wall quilt top.

Step 2. Use the remaining quilt binding to cover the ragged outer edge of the wall quilt. Pin one edge of the binding to the front of your quilt all the way around. Once again, you will be mitering the corners. As you come to each corner, fold the binding so it makes a little triangle of fabric under itself—just as you did earlier. Remember, this will make a diagonal seam at the corner—like on a picture frame. Pin each mitered corner in place as you go. When you have pinned the binding on all four sides, leave about 3" of extra binding at the end and cut off the rest.

Step 3. Using an appliqué stitch, sew the binding to the top of the quilt edge all the way around. Go back and sew each mitered corner separately.

Step 4. Pin the other edge of the binding to the back of the wall quilt and sew in place, using the same method you used above. To finish, cut the excess binding so there is only about 1" extra. Turn under ½" of this and stitch the folded end of the binding down to complete your wall quilt. Be sure to add your name and the date to the back.

Step 5. If you like, you can make fabric loops for hanging your wall quilt from the remaining quilt binding. Cut four 4" lengths of binding. Pin them to the top of the wall quilt so there is the same amount of space between each. Pin in place so that the ragged ends of the binding are folded and hidden underneath the binding itself. Then sew in place. A wooden dowel (available at most hardware stores) can be inserted through the loops for hanging your finished wall quilt.

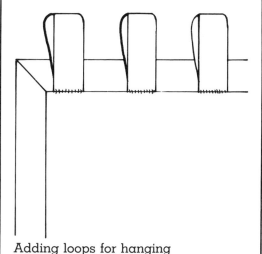

Adding loops for hanging

Autumn Leaves Wall Quilt

Please read chapter "13 About Doing Appliqué" before beginning this project.

The Maple Leaf has been a popular quilt pattern ever since New England women first started making quilts. There is a pieced Maple Leaf pattern and an appliquéd one. This project makes use of the appliquéd Maple Leaf.

There are two versions given for this project. The first version is for a wall quilt or crib quilt. Perhaps you know someone who would appreciate a handmade quilt for a baby's crib. Or maybe you'd like a wall hanging for yourself. Either way, you'll find Version 1 of this project to be a bit challenging, but not beyond your abilities.

The second version of this project involves much more time and effort. The pieced triangle border in particular takes a great deal of patience to complete. But if you've finished the other projects in this book and are ready for a real challenge, you might want to tackle it. Version 2 makes up into a large wall quilt. It could also be used as a small quilt for a single bed. If used on a bed, however, it will only come up to the bottom of the pillows, not cover them as most quilts are meant to do. Version 2 might be a good choice for you if your mother is a quilter and the two of you would enjoy working on a project together.

Both versions of this project combine three traditional quilt patterns—The Maple Leaf, The Schoolhouse, and The Bridal Wreath. Both versions call for many different colors of calico. Some colors are suggested in the directions, but you will want to choose your own. As mentioned in some of the earlier projects, you can often buy "quilter's quarters"—pre-cut quarter yards of calico for making quilts like this one. Keep in mind that your family and friends may be able to share fabric scraps with you. Check with your friends who sew or who have mothers and other relatives who sew, before buying bits of fabric. If you're lucky enough to have a friend who also quilts, the two of you will have fun trading fabric scraps.

When finished, the center wreath block of both versions of this project is a 14″ square. It can be made into a matching square pillow, using a standard 14″ square pillow form, to complement either version. It is a striking addition to any room to have a colorful wall hanging and a matching pillow in a nearby chair. To make the pillow, follow the directions for appliquéing the center block of Version 1. (It's the same for Version 2.) Then follow the directions for assembling the pillow from Project 2, The Pieced Pillow, in chapter 8.

Version 1

Materials

Quilt Blocks
2½ yards of white muslin
At least eight ¼-yard scraps of calico in reds, greens, and golds to make twelve autumn leaves, sixteen large hearts, and four schoolhouses

Center Wreath
One 6″ square of red calico for the small center heart
One ¼ yard of light blue calico for the small corner hearts
One ⅓ yard of light green calico for the wreath of leaves
One 15″ square of white muslin (may be cut from the above 2½ yards of muslin) for the center background block

Additional Materials
1 yard of 45″ wide batting
1 yard of 45″ wide muslin quilt backing fabric
Regular sewing thread to match all appliqué fabrics
Two 3-yard packages quilt binding to match one of the fabrics in the central block
Quilting thread

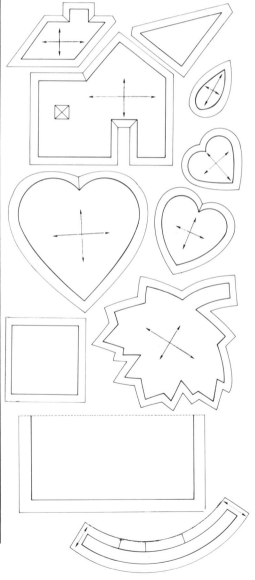

Tracing and Cutting

Step 1. There are seven templates for Version 1 of this project. They include the background block for the regular appliqué shapes, the maple leaf, the large heart, the schoolhouse, and, for the center wreath, a small heart, wreath leaf, and the wreath stem. Trace them all onto tracing paper. For each, you will be tracing a thin outer line and a thick inner line. The outer line will be your *cutting* line. The inner line will be a *folding* or *sewing* guide. For now, ignore the short, clipping lines on the templates between the cutting and folding lines. (Note that four of the wreath stem pieces put together make the wreath stem circle.)

Step 2. Turn over the tracing paper and lay it on the smooth side of a piece of fine sandpaper. Draw over the pattern lines to transfer them to the sandpaper below.

Step 3. Take away the tracing paper and darken the pattern lines on the sandpaper.

Step 4. With scissors, cut out the sandpaper templates along the *outer* lines you have drawn.

Step 5. For all the templates, lay out the fabrics you will be working with on a flat surface *right side down.* You will want to use your sandpaper template sand side down (or cardboard template right side down) to trace the cutting lines for all the appliqué shapes and blocks—except the leaves. When tracing the maple leaves, you may want to make half your leaves face one direction and half face the other direction, to give the feeling of falling leaves. To do this, trace half the maple leaves with your template *sand side down* and the other half with the template *sand side up.* (The same can be done with the schoolhouse template.)

Trace the following:

Quilt Blocks

      12 maple leaves
      16 large hearts
      4 schoolhouses
      32 8" square white background blocks

Center Wreath

      4 small blue hearts
      1 small red heart
      38 small leaves
      4 curved stems

Step 6. After you have traced all the shapes on fabric, re-cut your templates on their inner lines. Your new, re-cut templates should be ¼" smaller all the way around—except on the background blocks. These will have a ½" margin for sewing. (It is a little tricky to surround a large center block with smaller ones. This larger ½" margin on the blocks will help make your sewing easier.) Center each template on the correct fabric shape that you traced earlier. Then trace around the new, smaller template to mark your *folding* line on the appliqué shapes and your *sewing* line on the background blocks.

Step 7. Your appliqué shapes and blocks now have two lines around them. Cut them out on the outer *cutting* lines, leaving the inner lines for a folding or sewing guide.

Sewing the Design

Step 1. Iron all the cut-out fabric shapes and blocks—including the large center background block you cut out earlier.

Step 2. Take a look at the template drawings for this project. Remember the short clipping lines between the cutting and folding lines? Look at the drawings in the book and clip your appliqué shapes accordingly.

Step 3. To begin sewing the quilt blocks, take the first maple leaf in hand so the wrong side is facing you. Thread your "sharps" needle with a single, knotted strand of thread that matches the color of the first leaf. Use a short basting stitch to sew the folded edge of the leaf shape all the way around. Make the fold fall on the folding line that you drew earlier. After the first leaf is done, turn under and baste the remaining maple leaves and set them aside.

Step 4. Turn under and baste the large hearts just as you did the maple leaves. Do the same for the schoolhouses. Set each aside.

Step 5. Arrange and pin one appliqué (either a maple leaf, heart, or schoolhouse) on each background block.

Step 6. Once again, thread your needle with a single strand of knotted thread to match the appliqué shape you are working with. Sew the appliqués to the blocks, using an appliqué stitch. As each block is finished, set it aside.

Step 7. To begin sewing the center wreath block, turn under and baste the small hearts. Then do the same for the small wreath leaves. Be sure to use matching thread.

Step 8. To turn under and baste the circle of stems for the wreath, first sew the curved stems end to end to make a circle. (Remember to pin the stems with right sides together and sew from the back.) Fold under the inside edge of the circle you have made, using the folding line as a guide, and baste. Then fold and baste the outside edge of the circle.

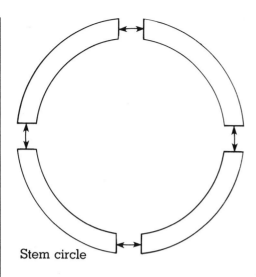

Stem circle

Step 9. Lay out the 15" square center background block. On one side of the fabric, use a ruler and pencil to mark a line ½" from the edges, all the way around. This will be your sewing line.

Center wreath

Step 10. Arrange the wreath circle, the leaves, and hearts on the 15" square block and pin them in place. You will have fewer leaves on the inside of the circle than on the outside.

Do not bring your appliqué shapes right to the edge of the pencil line you have drawn on the other side. You will want to leave a little extra space beyond the sewn edge of your center block.

Step 11. Sew the appliqué shapes in place as they have been pinned. Use a knotted, single strand of matching thread in your needle and sew with an appliqué stitch.

Setting the Quilt

Step 1. Iron all of the appliqué blocks you have sewn.

Version 1 piecing blocks

Step 2. On a large, flat surface (a clean swept floor may be best) lay out the ironed blocks exactly as they will appear in the finished quilt. The large center block will be in the middle, surrounded by the maple leaf blocks, with the hearts around the outside and the four schoolhouses in the corners.

Version 1 appliqué and piecing diagram

Step 3. As you sew the quilt blocks together, pay special attention to matching the seams correctly. To help you do this, sew the blocks into groups, rather than rows. Beginning with one of the four corners, sew four blocks into two pairs of blocks. Then sew these two pairs into a group of four blocks. Remember to line up the blocks being sewn with right sides together. Run your pin through the sewing lines to be sure the blocks are properly lined up.

As you finish sewing each group of four blocks, lay the group back in place on the work surface.

Step 4. When all the blocks are sewn into groups of four blocks each, begin joining these together using the same method you used above. This time, you will include the large center wreath block. Remember to match seams carefully as you go and to use your pin to help you line up the blocks before stitching.

Step 5. When all the blocks are joined into one large quilt top, iron the quilt top carefully.

Quilting the Project

Step 1. If you have not already done so, take a moment to read chapter "6 Quilting Makes the Quilt."

Step 2. On your large, flat work surface, place the muslin backing fabric *right side down*. Place the batting on top of it. (Note: most of the projects in this book suggest generous fabric and batting requirements. You will have only a small 1½" margin of extra backing fabric and batting beyond your quilt top, so *careful* placement at this point is very important.)

Place the ironed quilt top *right side up* on these and center it in place. There will be only a small margin of backing and batting sticking out beyond the edge of the quilt top but this amount should be even all the way around.

Step 3. Pin this quilt "sandwich" about every 6" or so to hold the layers together while you baste them.

Step 4. Use a contrasting color of thread to baste the "sandwich" layers in place. Take very long basting stitches—about 2" or 3" each. Use one line of basting up and down through the middle, a line of basting from left to right across the middle, a third line diagonally from the upper left corner to the lower right corner, and one line diagonally from the upper right corner to the lower left. Add basting as needed so that no area larger than 8" square is left unbasted.

Step 7. Put the quilt "sandwich" into the quilt hoop. You will want to quilt the center wreath first.

Schoolhouse, heart, and leaf blocks quilting diagram

Center wreath block quilting diagram

Step 8. Using a betweens quilting needle and heavy quilting thread, take tiny stitches around the outside of each appliqué shape. The line of stitching should be about ¼" away from the edge of each appliqué. Quilt a heart outline on the inside of all the heart appliqués.

Step 9. When you have finished quilting the center wreath, quilt the first row of blocks that goes all the way around it, next. You will have to replace your quilt "sandwich" in the hoop many times to reach all of the blocks. You will want to continue quilting from the center of the quilt toward the edges, finishing with the outer row of blocks. End your quilting stitches about 1" from the outer edges. When you have finished the quilting, remove your quilt from the hoop and take out the basting stitches.

Finishing Up

Step 1. Trim any extra batting and backing fabric to make them even with the edges of your quilt top.

Step 2. You will use the quilt binding to cover the ragged edge of the quilt. Pin one edge of the quilt binding to the front edge of your quilt all the way around. As you come to each corner, miter it; that is, fold the binding so it makes a little triangle of fabric under itself. This will make a diagonal seam show at the corner—like on a picture frame. (If you need help, please review "Binding the Quilt" from "6 Quilting Makes the Quilt.") Pin each mitered corner as you go. As you come to the end of one length of binding, join a new one to it. Cover the ragged end with the folded-over end of the new length of binding. Blind stitch in place. Continue pinning. When you have pinned the quilt binding on all four sides, cut the binding to leave 1" extra. Then turn under the edge of the very end of the binding and blind stitch it in place.

Step 3. Using an appliqué stitch, sew the quilt binding to the top of the quilt edge all the way around. Go back and sew each mitered corner separately.

Step 4. Turn the quilt over. Pin the other edge of the quilt binding to the back of the quilt and sew in place. Remember to add your name and the date on the back of your finished project.

Version 2

Version 2 of this project is considerably more difficult than Version 1. To make a large wall quilt like the photographed example of this project, you will have to follow the directions below in addition to completing the directions for Version 1.

Materials

You will need:
Additional calico fabric scraps to make 96 assorted-color triangles
Additional 2½ yards white muslin (1¼ yards to make 96 white border triangles, 1¼ yards to make 28 additional background blocks and the four tiny border corner squares)
Additional 15" square of light blue calico for the small border corner hearts
Additional fabric scraps and/or "quilter's quarters" (total of about 1½ yards) to make 20 additional maple leaves and 10 additional schoolhouses. *(Note: Version 2 calls for only 14 large hearts. That's two fewer hearts than in Version 1.)*

Tracing and Cutting

Step 1. Mark, trace, and cut out the following appliqués. Follow the same method for marking and cutting templates as well as fabric as in Version 1.

        32 maple leaves
        14 large hearts
        14 schoolhouses
        60 background blocks

Step 2. Mark, trace, and cut out templates and fabric for the center wreath block exactly as in Version 1. At the same time, mark and cut out fabric for four extra light blue hearts for the border corners.

Step 3. There are two additional templates included for Version 2—the border triangle, and the small white border corner block. Trace and cut out these templates for Version 2. Follow the same method as for the templates from Version 1. You will need 96 print triangles, 96 white triangles, and four tiny border corner blocks. Iron all the cut shapes.

Sewing the Design

Step 1. Clip all appliqués as indicated on the template drawings.

Step 2. Turn under and sew the edges of the maple leaf, large heart, and schoolhouse appliqués, using matching thread. Follow the same method as for the appliqué shapes in Version 1.

Step 3. Pin and sew one appliqué to each block, using matching thread and an appliqué stitch. Iron and organize your sewn blocks into three piles—one of maple leaves, one of hearts, and one of schoolhouses.

Step 4. Turn under and baste the appliqués for the large center wreath block. Pin the appliqués in place on the background block and appliqué. Iron and set aside.

Step 5. Turn under and baste each of the four small border corner hearts. Appliqué in place on the four tiny border corner blocks. Iron and set aside.

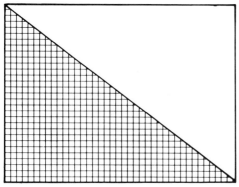
Two-triangle rectangle

Step 6. Before sewing the pieced triangle border, you may want to review "5 About Doing Pieced Work." Begin by joining all of the triangles into rectangles made up of one calico triangle and one white triangle each.

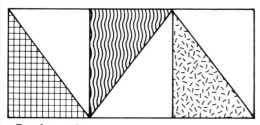
Border strip

Step 7. When all the triangles have been joined into rectangles, begin sewing the rectangles together into short strips of three rectangles each. Be sure that the triangles in the short strips alternate. That is, no two calico triangles and no two white triangles should fall next to each other. This will take a lot of patience. Be careful not to sew the short side of one rectangle to the long side of another rectangle. You will have 32 short border strips of three rectangles each when you are done. Iron each short strip and set aside.

Setting the Quilt

Step 1. Lay out the quilt blocks and border strips in the order they are to appear in the finished wall quilt. Pay careful attention to the diagram.

Step 2. Join the blocks into large rectangles of six blocks each. Note the diagram. Some of the groups will make up into horizontal rectangles. Others will make up into vertical rectangles.

Step 3. Join the large six-block rectangles and the center wreath block into the borderless quilt top. Follow the directions for Version 1 for matching seams.

Block and border strip with corner block

Step 4. Join the border strips to the outer edge of the quilt top—one strip to each block—except at the corners. You will need two short border strips for each corner block. When the short border strips have been sewn in place, sew the loose edge of each border strip to the strip next to it.

Version 2 appliqué and piecing diagram

Step 5. Pin and sew one of the corner heart blocks in each corner of the border.

Step 6. When all of the pieces of the quilt top (including the border) have been joined together, iron the quilt top as directed in Version 1.

Quilting the Project

Step 1. Follow the directions for quilting as in Version 1, quilting the additional appliqué blocks.

Step 2. Run a line of quilting ¼" inside each white triangle of the border. Quilt ¼" around the outside of each tiny heart in the corner blocks. You may find it is easier to quilt the border without the use of the quilting hoop.

Finishing Up

Step 1. Complete the project as directed for Version 1.

144

Glossary

Appliqué. Appliqué is a technique used in making some kinds of quilts. In appliqué, one piece of fabric is sewn (or "applied") onto a larger one. The ragged edges of the smaller piece of fabric are turned under or sewn under first, and then the piece is sewn or appliquéd onto the larger piece of fabric.

Appliqué stitch. An appliqué or blind stitch is used to sew the smaller piece of fabric onto the larger one in appliqué quiltmaking. This is a tiny stitch that is almost impossible to see. To make it especially hard to see, the quilter usually uses only one strand of thread that matches the smaller fabric piece exactly.

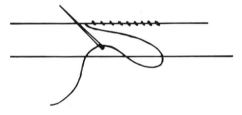

Basting stitch. This is a loose running stitch. It is used to hold fabric in place for a short while until more careful stitches can be taken. Small basting stitches are used to turn under a piece of fabric in appliqué. Long, loose basting stitches are used to hold the quilt top, batting, and quilt backing together while they are quilted.

Batting. The fluffy insides or filler of a quilt is called the batting. Today, quilt batting is usually made from cotton or polyester.

Betweens needles. *See* Needles.

Binding. The binding is the strip of fabric used to cover the ragged edges of a quilt or quilted item.

Blind stitch. *See* Appliqué stitch.

Block. A block is one unit of pieced or appliqué work in a quilt. Many blocks put together make up a whole quilt.

Bolt of fabric. New fabric usually comes wound around a large roll or flat bolt. Ask the clerk at the fabric store to cut off as much fabric as you need from the bolt.

Calico. Calico is a woven cotton fabric that has tiny flowers or some other very small print on it.

Colorfast. Fabric that is colorfast is dyed with permanent colors that will not run or fade when they get wet. Fabric that is not colorfast should never be used in any quiltmaking.

Cotton fabric. Regular cotton fabric has a firm weave, yet is light and easy to sew. It is especially good for making quilts.

Fabric grain. The fabric grain is the weave of the fabric. If you look closely at a piece of fabric, you will see that it is made up of many tiny threads going up, down, and across. "With the grain" means up and down or across—in the direction of these threads. "Against the grain" means not in the direction of the fabric threads.

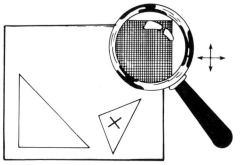

Fabric grain

Frame. *See* Quilting hoop.

Grain of the fabric. *See* Fabric grain.

Hoop. *See* Quilting hoop.

Matching seams. Seams between sewn pieces of fabric need to be lined up or matched in a continuous line as a quilt is put together.

Mitering the corners. As you sew binding on the edges of a quilt, you need to fold the binding at each corner. This makes a diagonal seam. The seam is called a miter and makes the quilt corner look a little like the corner on a picture frame.

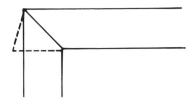

Muslin. A white cotton fabric that is lightweight and easy to sew.

Needles. You will use two kinds of needles in making a quilt. Betweens needles are short and are used for quilting. Sharps needles are long and are used for regular sewing.

Pieced work or piecing. Pieced work refers to small pieces of cloth sewn together in a geometric pattern to make a quilt block or a quilt. When you do this kind of sewing, you are piecing a quilt.

Preshrunk. Fabric that is preshrunk will not get smaller when it gets wet or is washed. You can buy preshrunk fabric or you can preshrink fabric yourself by washing it. Fabric that is not preshrunk should never be used in quiltmaking.

Quilt top. The pretty pieced or appliquéd top layer of a quilt is the quilt top.

Quilt backing. The fabric on the back of a quilt is called the quilt backing. The batting is the middle layer between the top and backing of a quilt.

Quilting. The quilting in a quilt refers to the tiny stitches used to hold the three layers of the quilt together.

Quilting hoop. This is a large pair of wooden circles that hold a quilt flat while you sew the quilting stitches in place. A quilting frame may be used to do the same thing, but it is much larger and takes up more room. Many quilters can sit around a quilting frame at the same time.

Running stitch. A running stitch is a basic up-and-down stitch. It is used to make a line of stitching.

Seam. The line of stitching that joins two pieces of fabric together is called the seam.

Setting. Setting a quilt means sewing together the blocks or units of the quilt in the way they are finally meant to appear.

Sharps. *See* Needles.

Solid cotton. The word "solid" is used in this book to describe a fabric that is only one single (or solid) color.

Template. A template is a pattern guide. It is made of cardboard, sandpaper, or some other sturdy, stiff material that will last even though it is used many times. There are two kinds of templates in quilt making. Pattern templates are used for cutting out fabric pieces. Quilting templates are used as a guide in sewing quilting stitches. In this book, the pattern templates all have two outlines. The quilting templates all have one outline.

Template Section

Pieced Potholder
Square

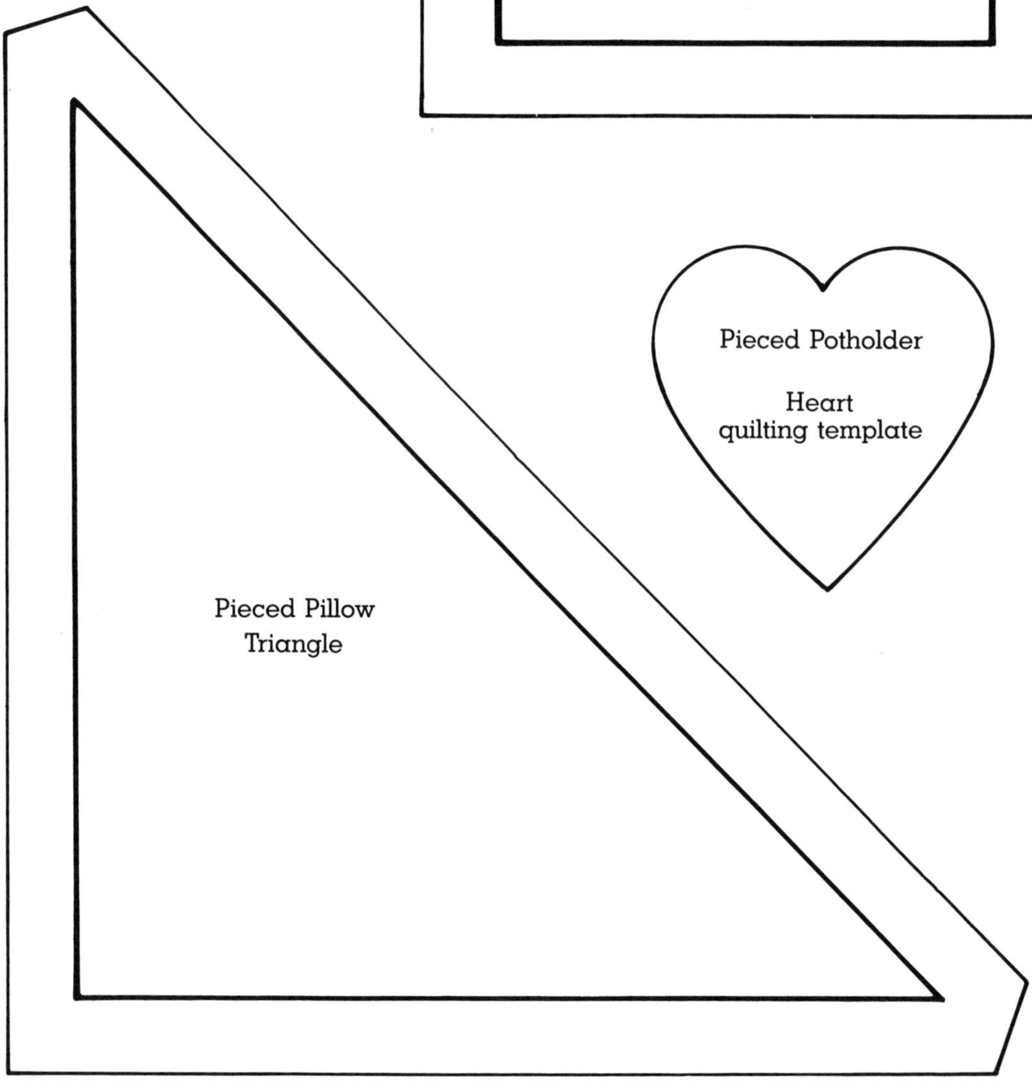

Pieced Potholder

Heart
quilting template

Pieced Pillow
Triangle

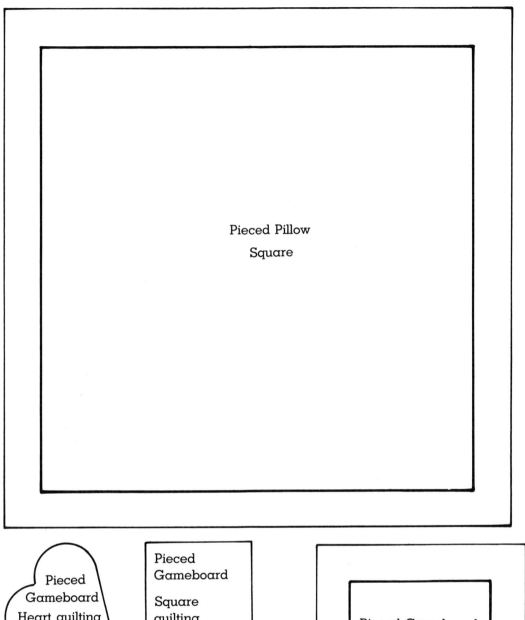

Pieced Pillow
Square

Pieced
Gameboard
Heart quilting
template

Pieced
Gameboard

Square
quilting
template

Pieced Gameboard
Square

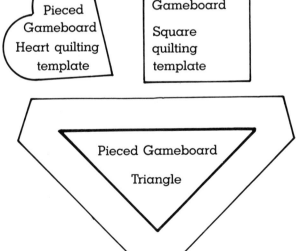

Pieced Gameboard

Triangle

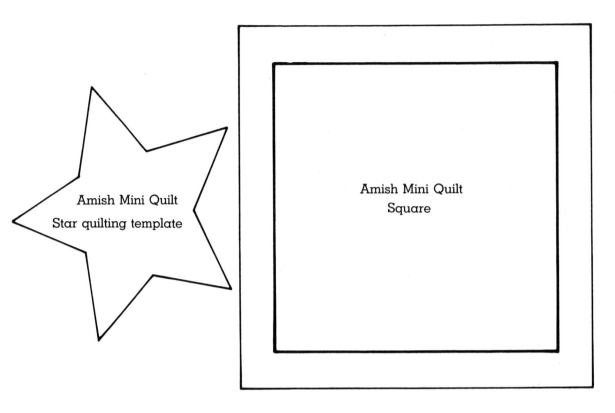

Amish Mini Quilt
Star quilting template

Amish Mini Quilt
Square

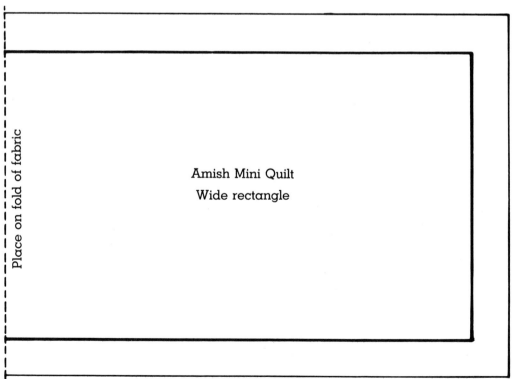

Place on fold of fabric

Amish Mini Quilt
Wide rectangle

150

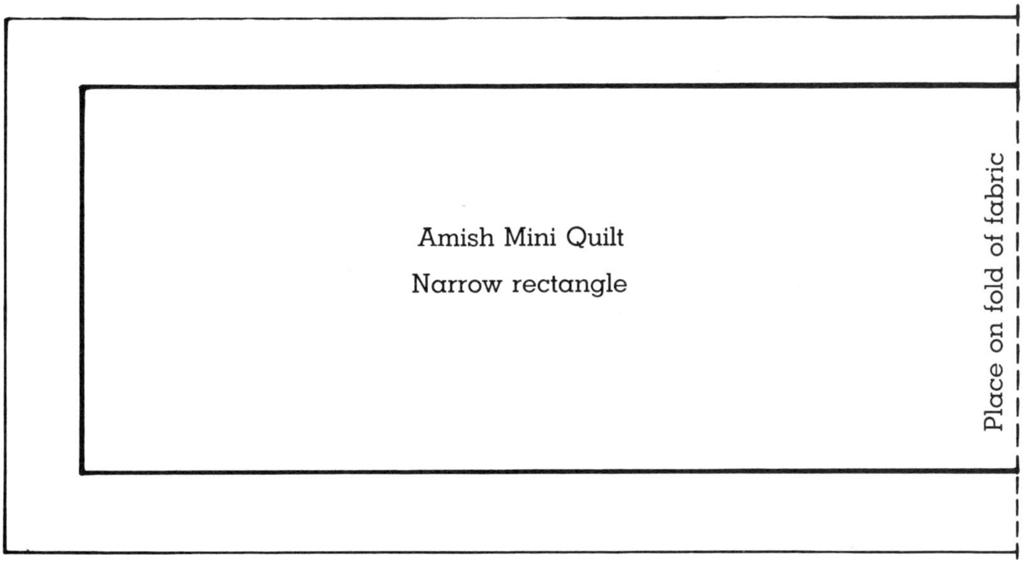

Amish Mini Quilt

Narrow rectangle

Place on fold of fabric

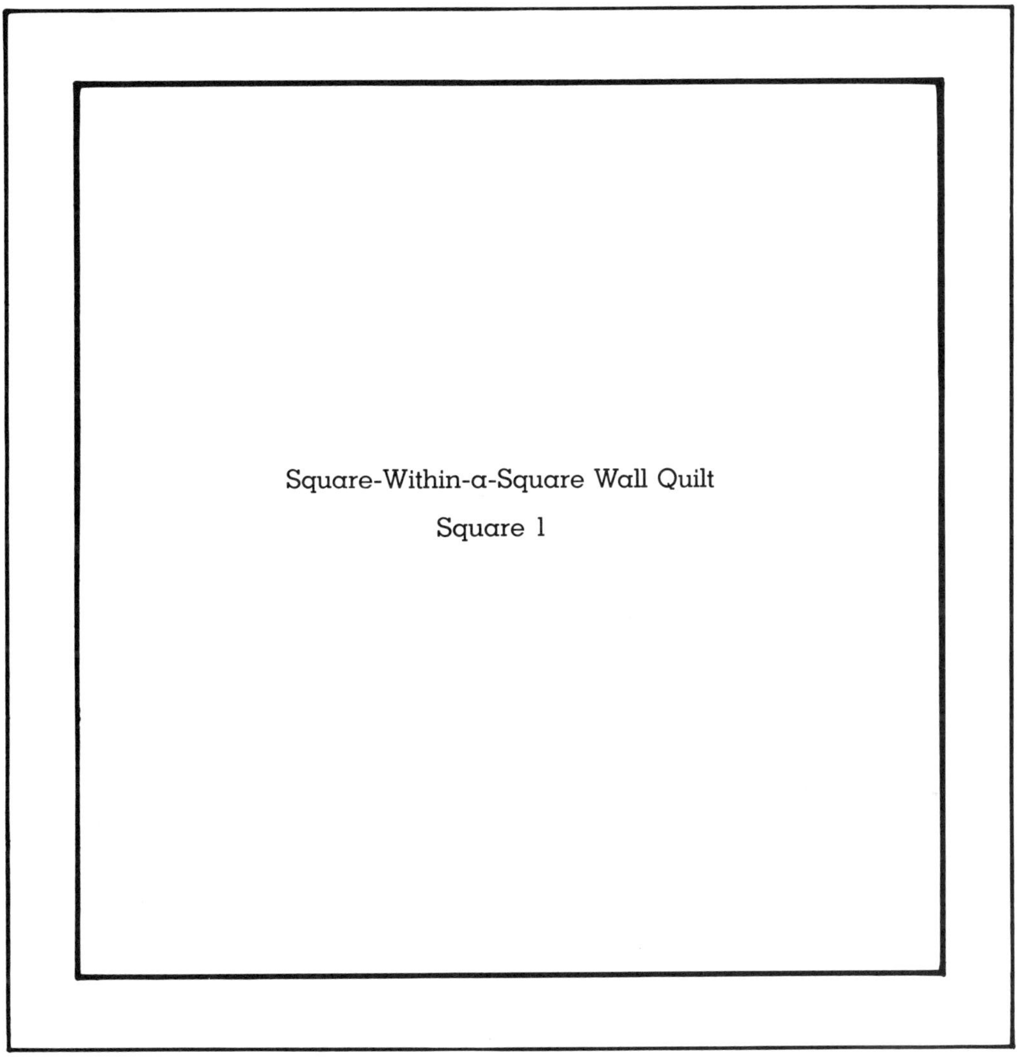

Square-Within-a-Square Wall Quilt

Square 1

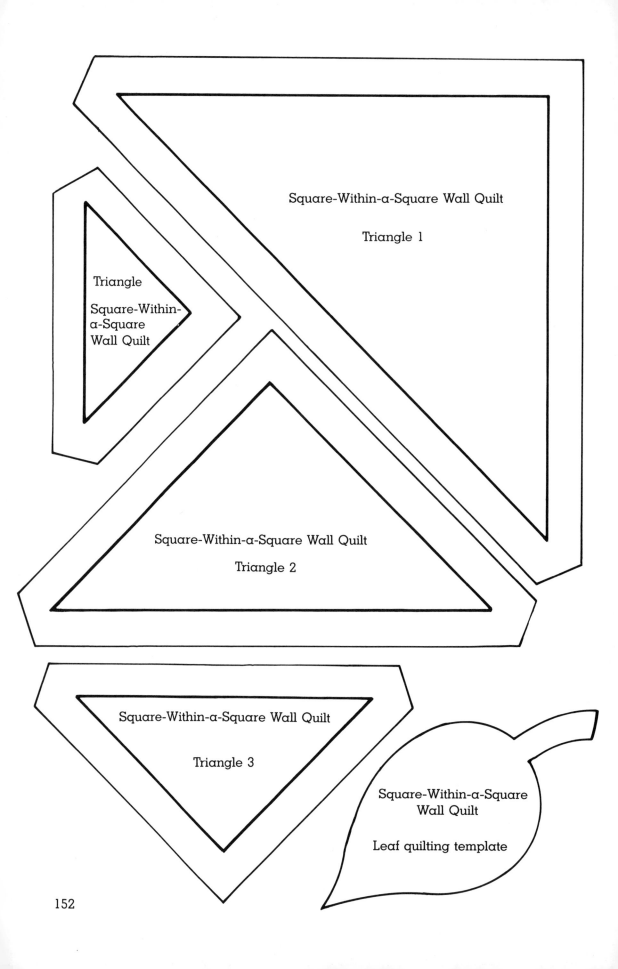

Square-Within-a-Square Wall Quilt

Triangle 1

Triangle
Square-Within-a-Square Wall Quilt

Square-Within-a-Square Wall Quilt

Triangle 2

Square-Within-a-Square Wall Quilt

Triangle 3

Square-Within-a-Square Wall Quilt

Leaf quilting template

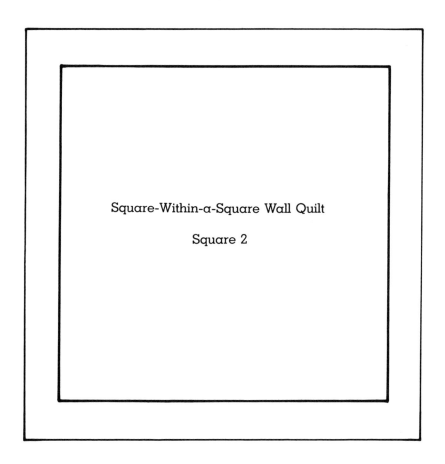

Square-Within-a-Square Wall Quilt

Square 2

Bear's Paw Quilt
Rectangle

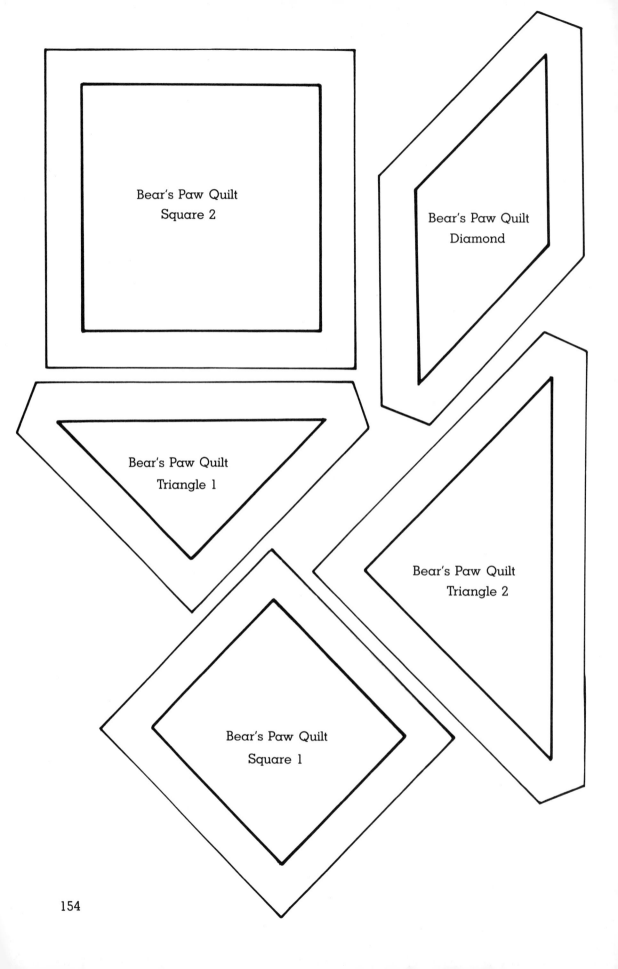

Bear's Paw Quilt
Square 2

Bear's Paw Quilt
Diamond

Bear's Paw Quilt
Triangle 1

Bear's Paw Quilt
Triangle 2

Bear's Paw Quilt
Square 1

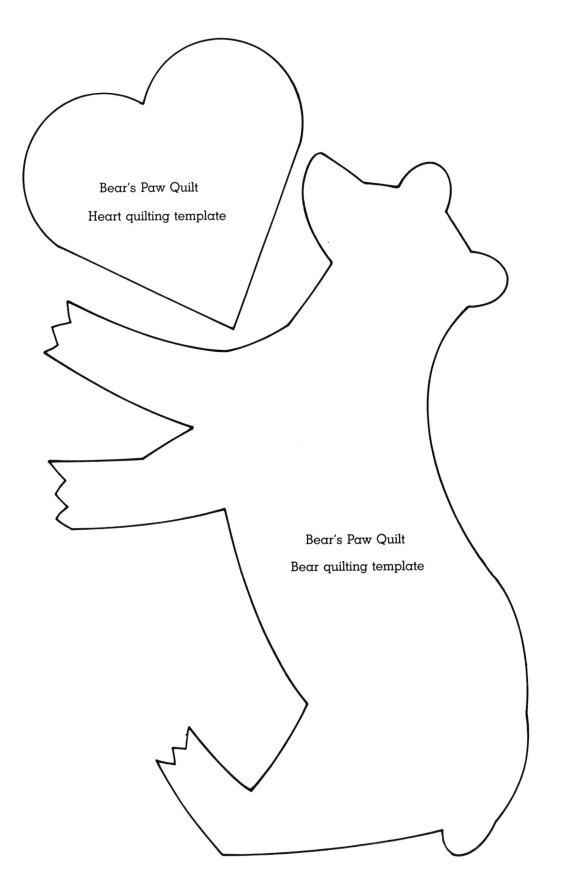

Bear's Paw Quilt

Heart quilting template

Bear's Paw Quilt

Bear quilting template

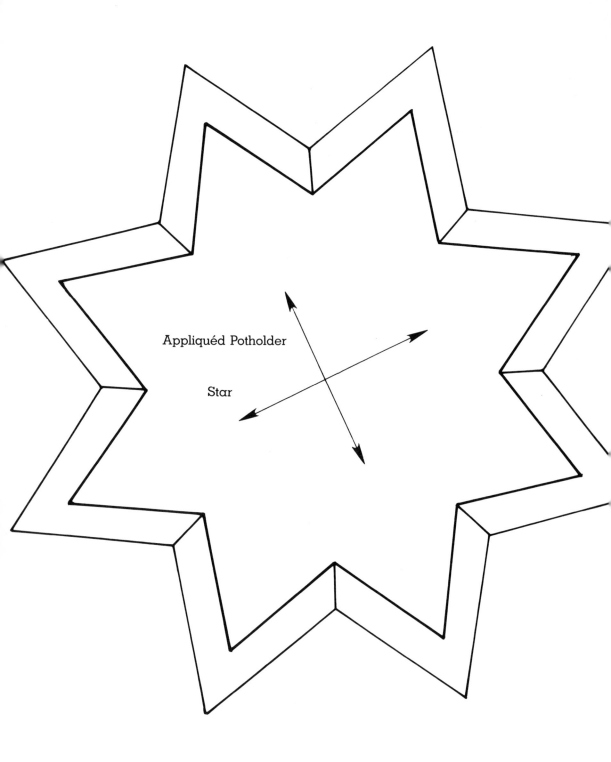

Appliquéd Potholder

Star

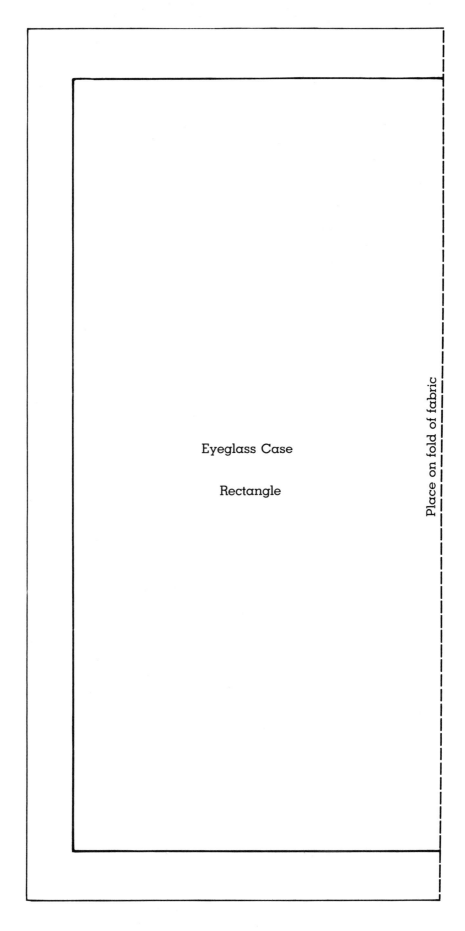

Eyeglass Case

Rectangle

Place on fold of fabric

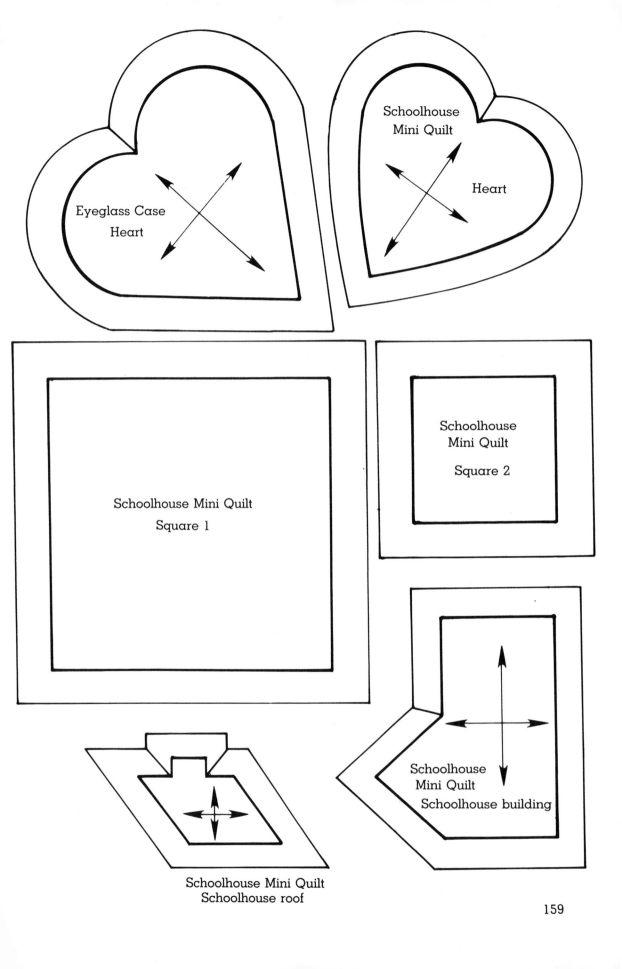

Eyeglass Case
Heart

Schoolhouse
Mini Quilt

Heart

Schoolhouse Mini Quilt
Square 1

Schoolhouse
Mini Quilt

Square 2

Schoolhouse
Mini Quilt

Schoolhouse building

Schoolhouse Mini Quilt
Schoolhouse roof

159

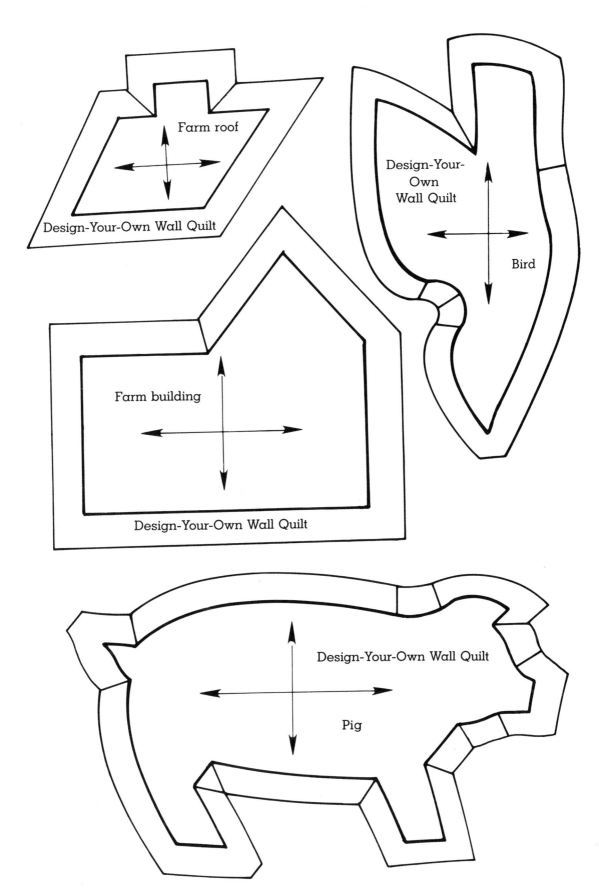

Farm roof

Design-Your-Own Wall Quilt

Design-Your-Own Wall Quilt

Bird

Farm building

Design-Your-Own Wall Quilt

Design-Your-Own Wall Quilt

Pig

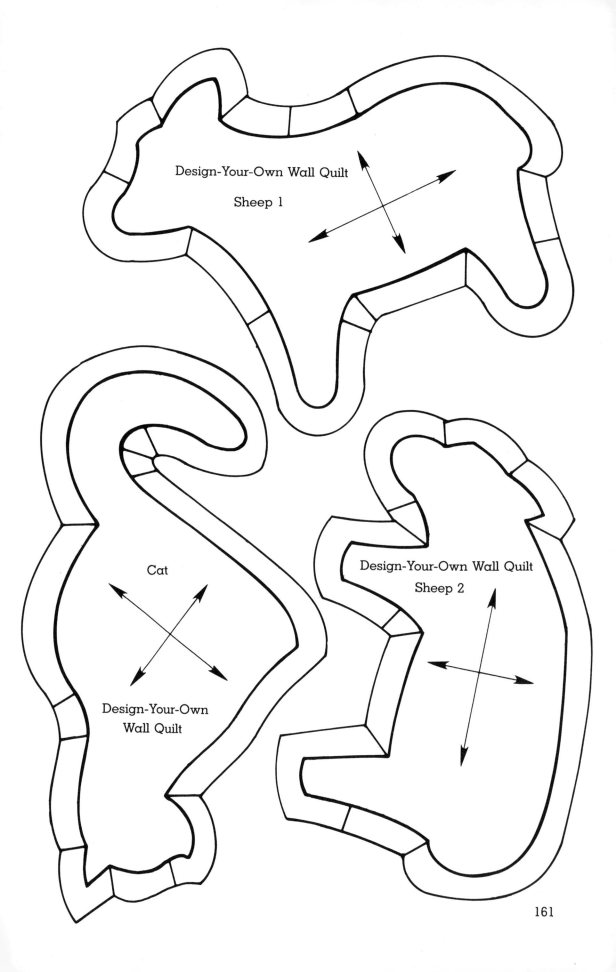

Design-Your-Own Wall Quilt

Sheep 1

Cat

Design-Your-Own
Wall Quilt

Design-Your-Own Wall Quilt

Sheep 2

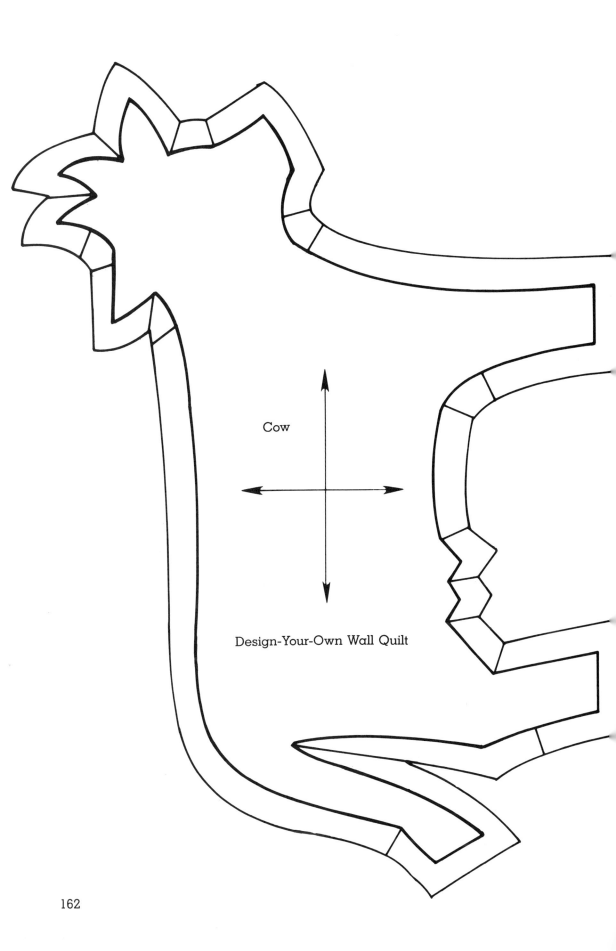

Cow

Design-Your-Own Wall Quilt

162

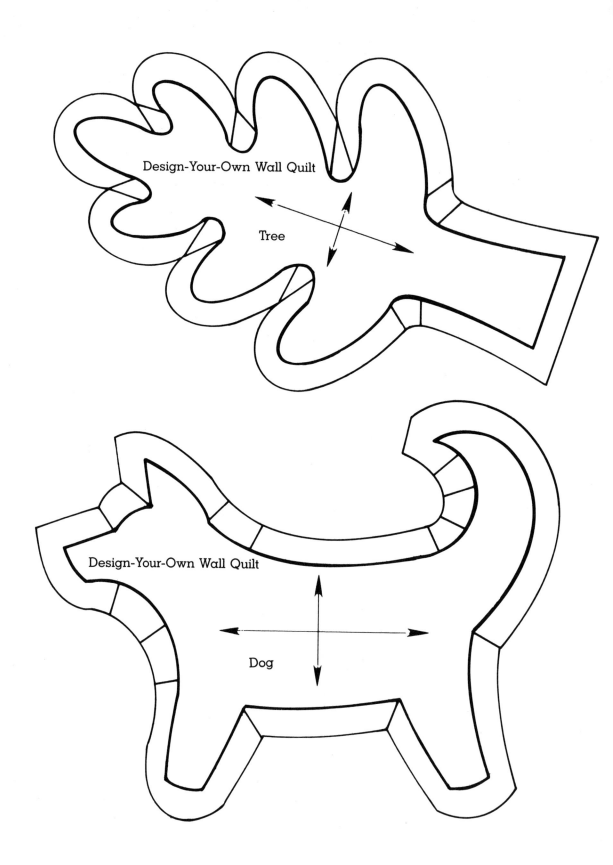

Design-Your-Own Wall Quilt

Tree

Design-Your-Own Wall Quilt

Dog

163

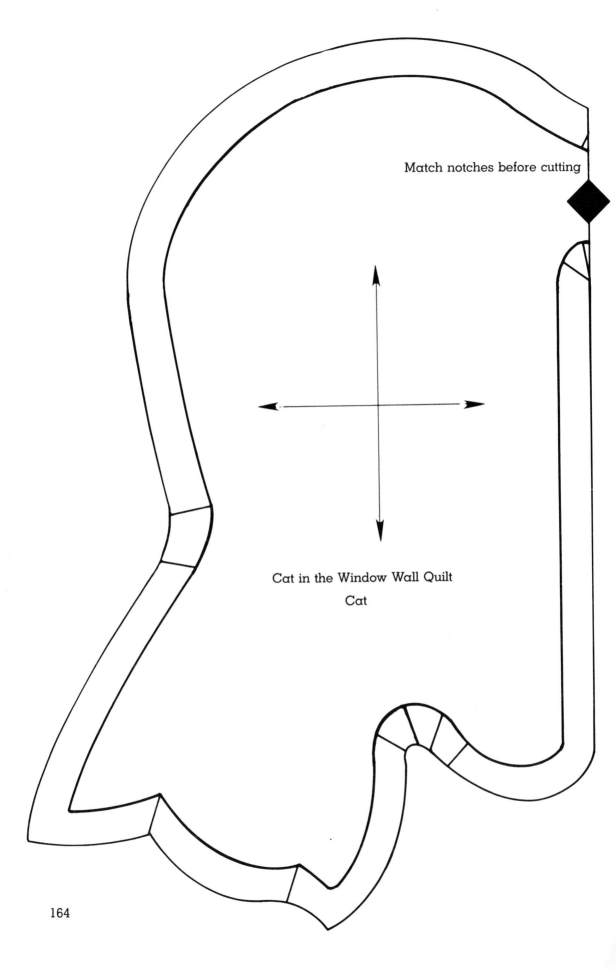

Match notches before cutting

Cat in the Window Wall Quilt

Cat

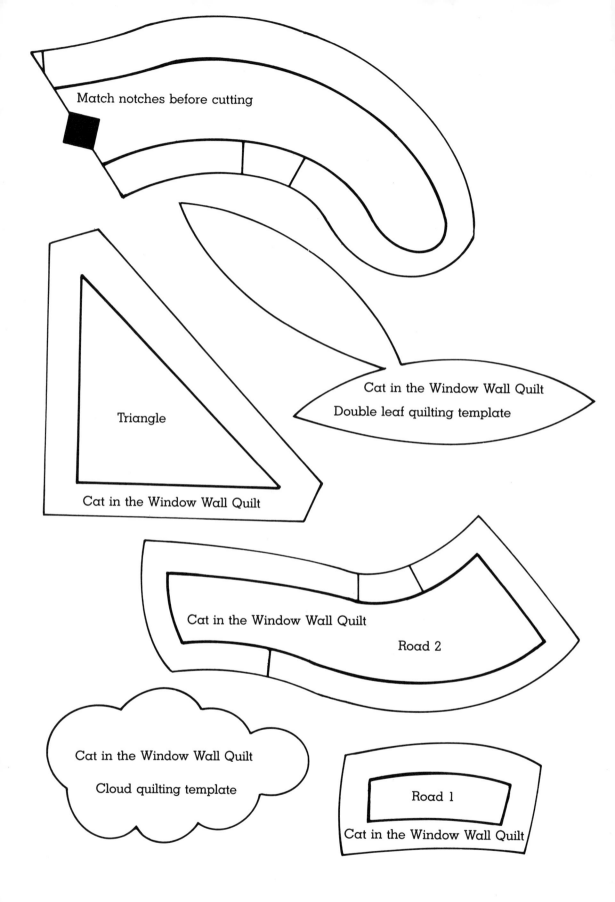

Match notches before cutting

Triangle

Cat in the Window Wall Quilt

Cat in the Window Wall Quilt

Double leaf quilting template

Cat in the Window Wall Quilt

Road 2

Cat in the Window Wall Quilt

Cloud quilting template

Road 1

Cat in the Window Wall Quilt

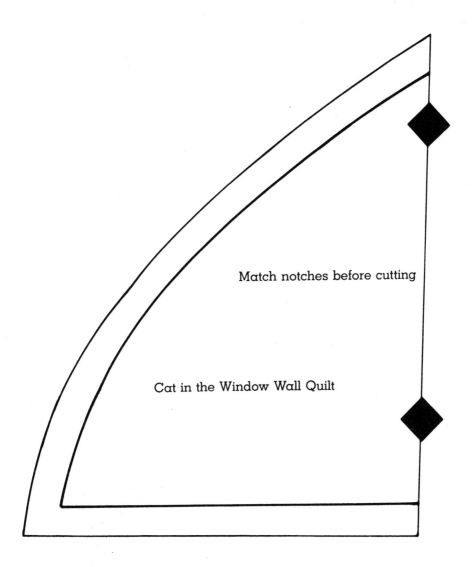

Match notches before cutting

Cat in the Window Wall Quilt

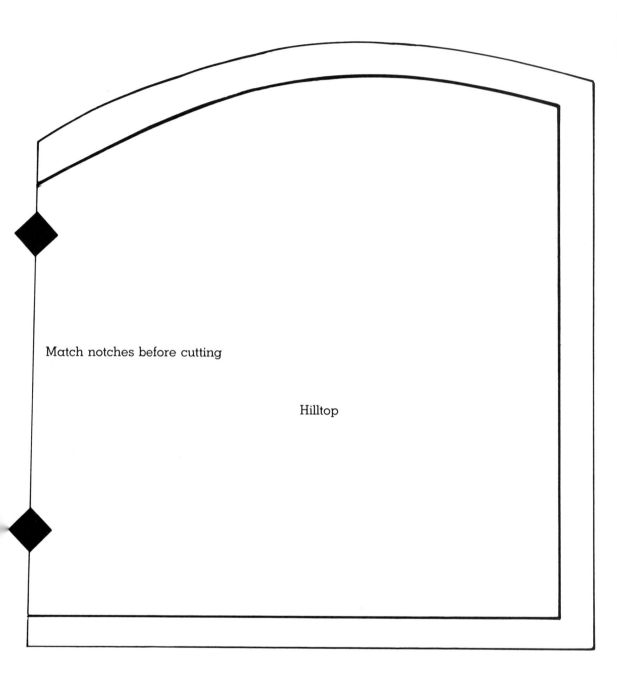

Match notches before cutting

Hilltop

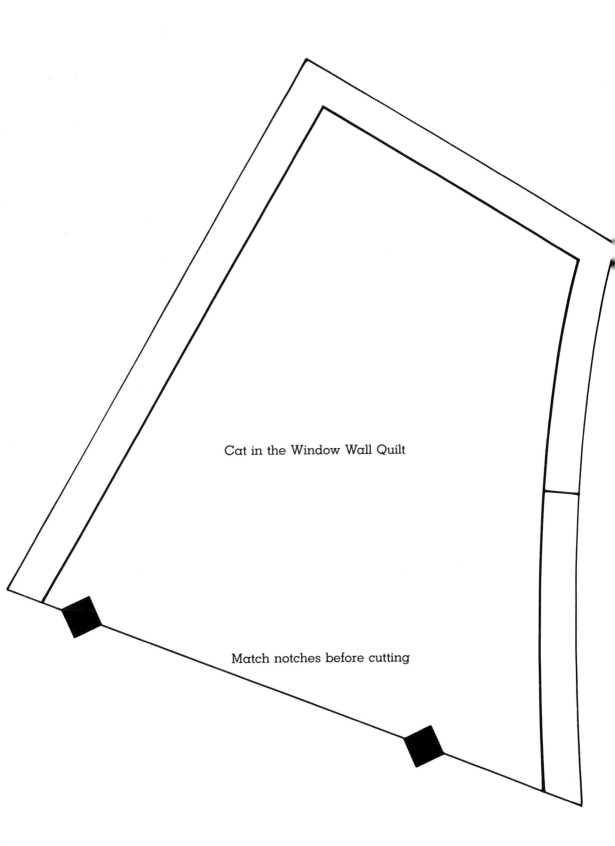

Cat in the Window Wall Quilt

Match notches before cutting

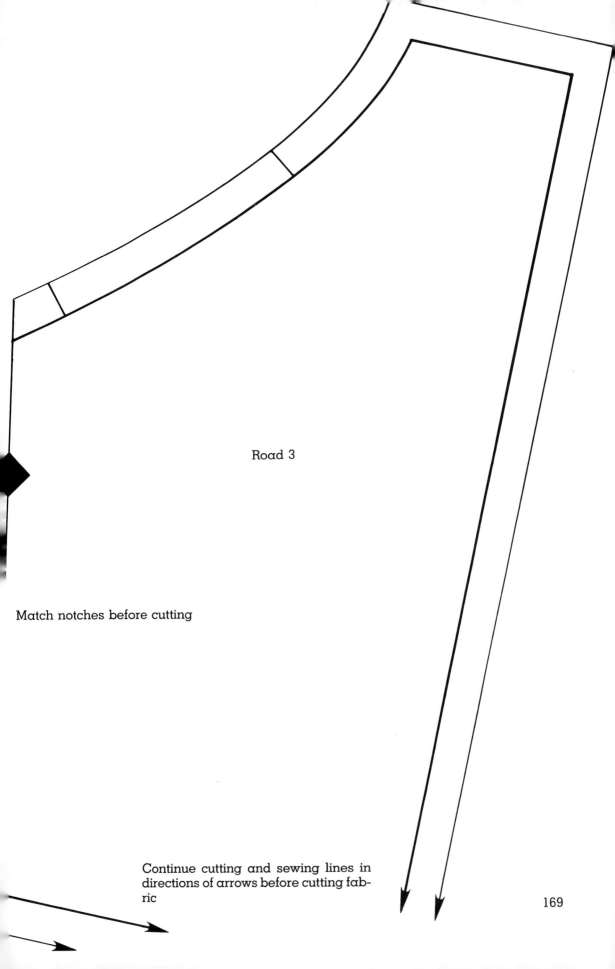

Road 3

Match notches before cutting

Continue cutting and sewing lines in directions of arrows before cutting fabric

169

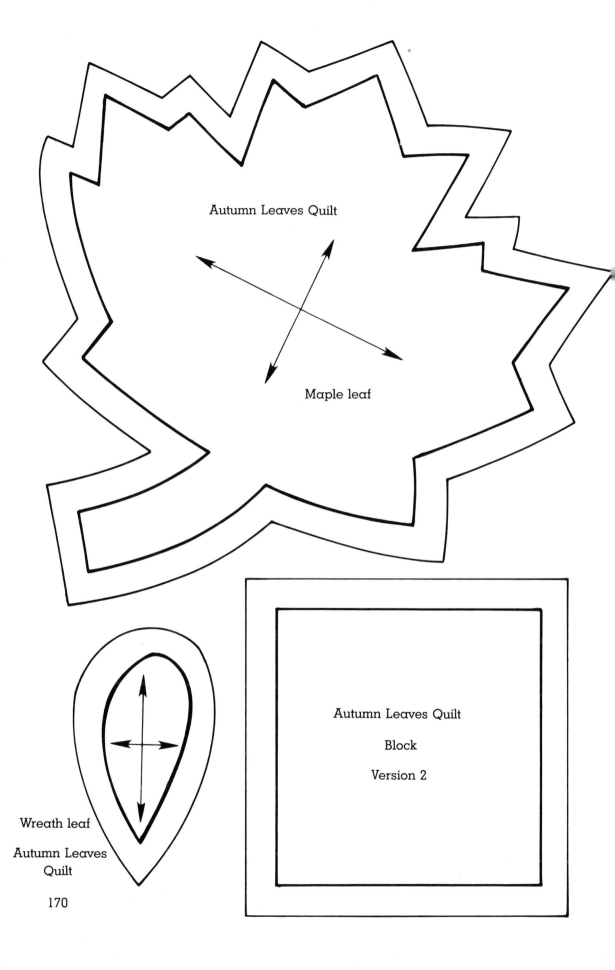

Autumn Leaves Quilt

Maple leaf

Wreath leaf

Autumn Leaves
Quilt

Autumn Leaves Quilt

Block

Version 2

170

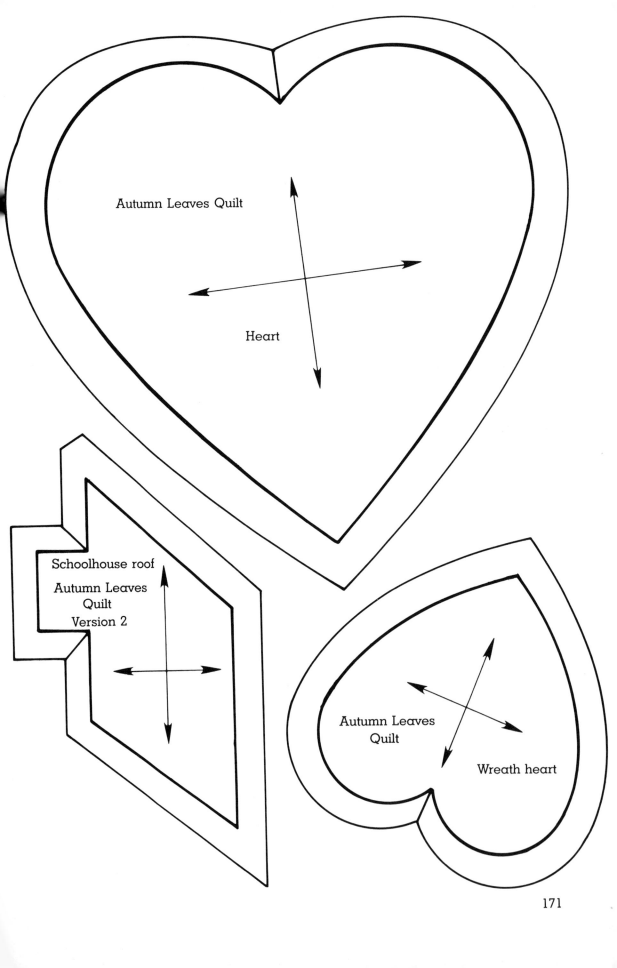

Autumn Leaves Quilt

Heart

Schoolhouse roof

Autumn Leaves
Quilt
Version 2

Autumn Leaves
Quilt

Wreath heart

171

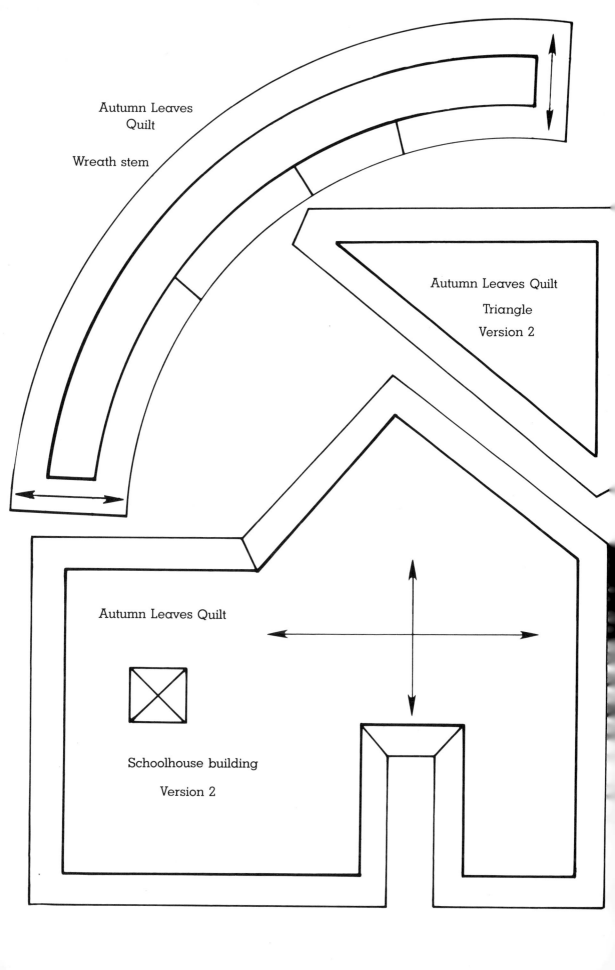

Autumn Leaves
Quilt

Wreath stem

Autumn Leaves Quilt

Triangle

Version 2

Autumn Leaves Quilt

Schoolhouse building

Version 2

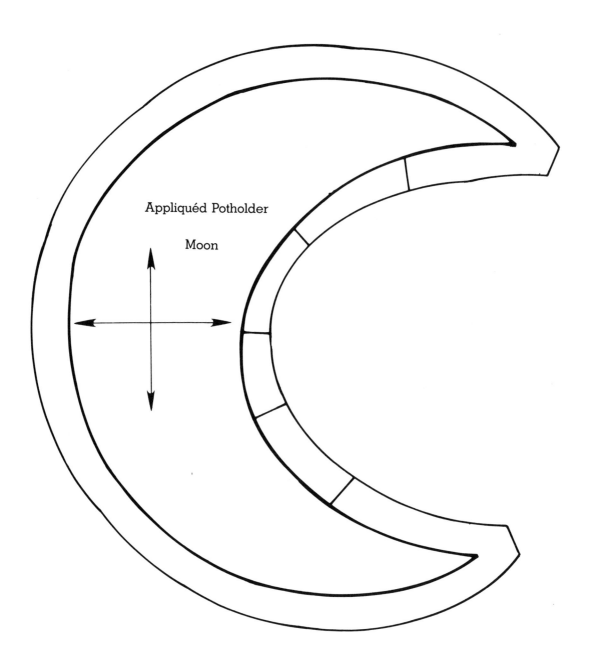

Appliquéd Potholder

Moon

157

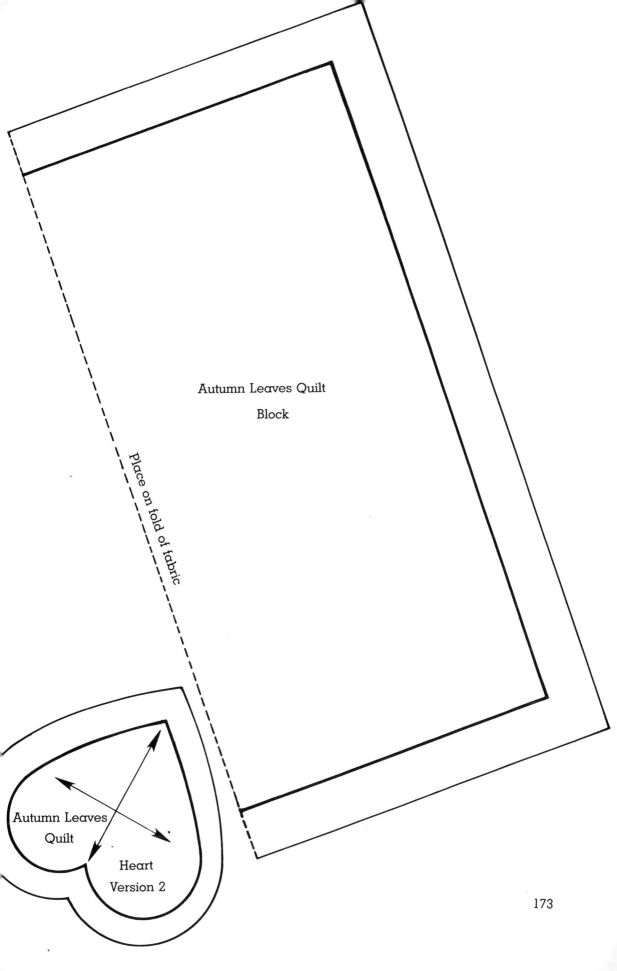

Autumn Leaves Quilt

Block

Place on fold of fabric

Autumn Leaves
Quilt

Heart
Version 2

Index

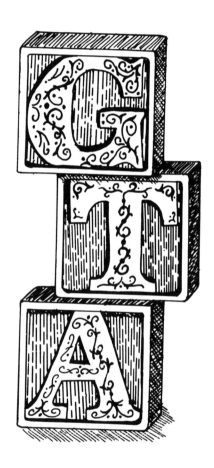

About the Author

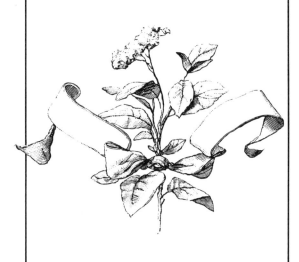

Willow Ann Soltow is a writer and quiltmaker who lives in New York State with her husband Ted and their cat Blue—who served as the model for one of the projects in this book. Willow enjoys writing for young people and helping them learn to express themselves through quiltmaking as well as other crafts. She is a graduate of Brown University.